DERBY COUNTY

PLAYER OF THE YEAR **1969–2008**

DERBY COUNTY
PLAYER OF THE YEAR 1969–2008
JIM FEARN

First published in Great Britain in 2008 by
The Breedon Books Publishing Company Limited
Breedon House, 3 The Parker Centre, Derby, DE21 4SZ.

This paperback edition published in Great Britain in 2013
by DB Publishing, an imprint of JMD Media Ltd

ISBN 978-1-78091-382-7

Printed and bound in the UK by Copytech (UK) Ltd Peterborough

CONTENTS

Introduction

There was an agreeable symmetry to the moment as, just before kick-off at the last game of the 2007–08 Premier League season, the public address system at Pride Park Stadium introduced the Derby County legend who would be making the presentation of the Jack Stamps Player of the Year Trophy. As Roy McFarland strode onto the pitch, trophy in hand, to tumultuous applause from the Derby faithful, arguably the club's greatest living former player might have recalled a memory from exactly 39 years earlier when his own name was announced as the first-ever winner of the very same trophy.

At the end of the 1968–69 season – McFarland's second with the Rams and also the second campaign orchestrated by the club's outspoken and brilliant young manager Brian Clough – there was an air of optimism among Derby County fans as their club returned to the top flight for the first time in 16 years. These faithful fans had been starved of success since two goals from centre-forward Jack Stamps had helped Derby to a 4–1 victory over Charlton Athletic at Wembley Stadium as the Rams won the first post-war FA Cup in 1946, the first trophy of any importance since the club's foundation way back in 1884.

On his appointment as manager in the summer of 1967, Clough inherited a crowd-thrilling future Player of the Year in striker Kevin Hector and already had on the books two dependable defenders, Ron Webster and Peter Daniel, who would also be Jack Stamps Trophy recipients in coming seasons. Clough and his right-hand man Peter Taylor added the key components of a side that not only won the Second Division Championship at a canter but also went on to win the First Division title, the equivalent of today's Premier League.

Arriving at the splendidly ramshackle Baseball Ground in the Clough and Taylor years were the likes of John O'Hare, Alan Hinton, Archie Gemmill, Dave Mackay, Colin Todd and, of course, McFarland. Of these, only Hinton missed out on the Jack Stamps Trophy – a trophy awarded on the basis of a fans' vote.

O'Hare was Player of the Year as Derby adjusted easily to life in the top flight in 1969–70, while the team's inspirational leader Mackay, proving he could still strut his stuff with the best in the business, took the honour in 1970–71. The following season Clough and Taylor's Derby were League champions for the first time and the sublime Todd, who was Mackay's replacement as McFarland's partner at the heart of the Rams' defence, was the overwhelming choice as Player of the Year.

Crowd hero Hector, who would eventually make more appearances for Derby than any other player, finally received Player of the Year recognition in 1973, and another stalwart, Webster, was the choice in 1974 at the end of a turbulent season that saw Clough and Taylor resign in acrimonious circumstances, to be replaced as manager by the only man on the planet who could have commanded the respect of a disenchanted dressing room, the returning Mackay.

Unwittingly, McFarland was responsible for the supporters' choice of Player of the Year at the end of the club's second First Division-winning season in 1974–75. A ruptured Achilles tendon on international duty with England ruled out the country's most talented defender for almost an entire season and opened the door for the dependable Daniel, a perennial reserve player who played out of his skin alongside the magnificent Todd. Todd was undoubtedly Derby's best player during the season in which stand-in skipper Gemmill lifted the League Championship Trophy, but Rams fans love players such as Daniel, who never shirk and always give their all. Twenty-one years later, as Jim Smith's team celebrated promotion to the Premier League for the first time, another no-frills defender, Dean Yates, was the supporters' choice as Player of the Year despite the more obvious claims of the motivational Igor Stimac (though the quirky Croatian, the catalyst as Smith's team were transformed from zeroes to heroes, will swear he *was* voted Player of the Year in 1995–96).

Among the Jack Stamps Trophy winners whose achievements with Derby earned them legendary status, names of distinction such as Charlie George, Bobby Davison, Mark Wright, Dean Saunders, Ted McMinn and, more recently, popular goalkeeper Mart Poom, are the 'honest Joe' performers such as David Langan, Roger Jones, Ross MacLaren, Chris Powell and Youl Mawéné. Ask any Derby fan and they will tell you that is just how it should be.

The supporters, though, faced probably their most difficult Player of the Year choice as a dismal 2007–08 drew to a close. A year after top scorer Steve Howard had become the latest winner of the Jack Stamps Trophy as Billy Davies's team headed for Wembley Play-off glory, Rams supporters were asked to nominate the best performer in a side that won only one League game throughout the entire 2007–08 season and racked up a succession of unwanted Premier League records.

While defender Darren Moore, a trier to the last, scooped an unofficial Player of the Year title voted by a panel of local journalists, the supporters, universally judged the best in the League for the way they stuck by their team through thin and thinner, voted themselves in as the 2007–08 Player of the Year. Though not to everyone's tastes (some pointed out there had been similarly disastrous seasons in the previous 39 years but always an actual *player* chosen as Player of the Year), it was a choice keenly supported by the new American owners of Derby County.

So it was that McFarland strode onto the Pride Park pitch as the Rams prepared to take on Reading, another club destined for relegation, symbolically holding aloft the Jack Stamps Trophy for the supporters themselves to savour.

* * *

I make no apology for claiming the idea to invite McFarland to make this mock 'presentation' as my own. In times of current turmoil there is nothing like a dollop of nostalgia to charm the supporters, and Roy Mac is rightly guaranteed a generous reception whenever he chooses to visit Pride Park Stadium.

He was in the Derby side on Boxing Day 1970 when I saw my first-ever match at the Baseball Ground. My uncle, David Fearn, had two season tickets in the Ley Stand and decided that, at the age of nine and with a worrying inclination towards Matt Busby's star-studded Manchester United, it was about time his noisy nephew was introduced to the home of the mighty Rams to witness at first hand Brian Clough's black-and-white revolution.

We all remember our journeys to the Baseball Ground. Mine always started at Matlock Railway Station, waiting with a handful of hardy Rams fans on the rather stark and scruffy station platform for the Derby train to trundle in. It is a 30-minute journey with six stops; first Matlock Bath, then on to Cromford, Whatstandwell and Ambergate, and at each station more supporters and their black-and-white scarves would be collected. Belper Station always doubled the growing band, and after one last stop at Duffield the train arrived at the dark and rather forbidding Derby Station, with its echoing announcements to places I had never heard of, let alone visited, 'Loughborough, Market Harborough, Kettering, Luton…'

Then was the walk up Midland Road and the left turn into London Road, which in the early 1970s was a mix of shops and housing, some derelict and some undergoing demolition. It was here that a brick flew inches past my head, smashing the shop window behind me as I hurried back to the station after Kevin Hector's testimonial match against Nottingham Forest. Happy days!

From London Road into Bateman Street, where, after I became a regular fan in my stack-heeled shoes, I still had to step over the puddles to avoid my too-long A-shaped beige Oxford bags getting wet around the turn-ups. Then crossing Osmaston Road, off into Douglas Street, where Derby fans taking a more leisurely trip to the Baseball Ground raucously spilled out onto the streets from tiny pubs with pints of ale in hand. While the sense of anticipation increased with each step, it was not until you turned the corner from Dairy House Road into Cambridge Street that the real thrill of match day gripped you for the first time. The throng of fans, the floodlights, the smell of fish and chips, the street sellers with programmes, rosettes and scarves. The Baseball Ground.

Everyone headed in the same direction towards Shaftesbury Crescent – the impossibly narrow road between the main stand wall and the terraced housing opposite which in later years was demolished in favour of a Derby County staff car park. I remember the opportunist householders who opened up their front windows to sell sweets. I would always queue at one window in particular for a quarter of Halls Mentol Lyptus drops.

Then on down Shaftesbury Crescent past the main stand Directors' Entrance where I waited after matches, autograph book in hand, before turning left just before the Baseball Hotel into Vulcan Street, then across the back of the Normanton stand to the Ley Stand turnstiles.

The *Match of the Day* cameras were in residence on that first day I saw Derby play; it was Boxing Day 1970, and snow covered the pitch. The opposition were Manchester United, and in Brian Clough's side were seven players who it has been my pleasure to interview for this book – all eventual winners of the Jack Stamps Trophy. If George Best, who scored one of United's four goals that day past Les Green (it was the goalkeeper's last game for the Rams) was my hero going into the game, Kevin Hector, who also scored one of Derby's four, was my new hero as I walked away in a daze with 34,000 others who had also witnessed a remarkable match between the audacious Clough's developing Derby and Matt Busby's European champions of just two years before. United had fielded not only Best, but also Law and Charlton. I could not quite believe these superstars were really here, in Derby, at the Baseball Ground, in the red of Manchester United. I watched awestruck from my seat in the new Ley Stand, an early monument to Clough's Rams revolution, while the Popsiders roared in the terracing below, Bobby Charlton took corners and goals flowed at either end.

For the record, the seven Players of the Year included in this book in the Derby side that day were Ron Webster, Peter Daniel, Roy McFarland, Dave Mackay, John O'Hare, Kevin Hector and Archie Gemmill.

If anyone had told the excited nine-year-old making his way back down Dairy House Road from his first Rams match that one day he would actually interview these players for a book, he would most probably have choked on his Menthol Lyptus drop.

1968–69 **Roy McFarland**

It was an iconic moment and every follower of English football, including those not even born when it happened, knows the story. Toddlers at the time too young to fully appreciate its significance, years later still have a vague recollection of a scarf, a rattle, a black-and-white television set, dad in tears and a celebration to end all celebrations. But if you were a teenager in the summer of 1966, you lived it.

There was surely no better time to be a football-mad youngster than during that summer of England's World Cup victory. In his native Liverpool, where the clubs and bars in pop music's capital were reverberating to the strains of *Paperback Writer*, Lennon and McCartney's 10th consecutive number-one hit, another Macca had just signed his first professional football contract.

Had you told Tranmere Rovers' latest recruit that within five years he would be playing in the famous shirt of England with the three lions crest alongside World Cup winners Gordon Banks, Bobby Moore, Alan Ball, Martin Peters and hat-trick hero Geoff Hurst, he would have laughed in your face.

Roy McFarland – arguably second only to the legendary Steve Bloomer in Derby County's list of all-time greats – was a reluctant recruit to football. At the age of 18 he was perfectly happy with his chosen career, having just been promoted after almost two years as a trainee accountant; however, it turned out to be a useful background years later when told by Derby County's chairman his first job as manager was to raise £6 million!

'I got into football by the back door,' Roy tells me with a wry smile. 'It's over 40 years since I started, and I don't regret one moment since the day I signed on for Tranmere Rovers in 1966.'

Roy Mac admits that before Tranmere came in for him, he never really took football seriously – not as a career at any rate – but like any Liverpudlian raised in the 1950s and early 1960s, he played football every spare moment. 'Liverpool in those days was like Coronation Street,' he tells me. 'There were no cars, and we kicked a ball against the school wall, which was next-but-one to my house. With a football or tennis ball, that's probably the best practice any youngster can get. Dad didn't get home until 7 o'clock most nights; he worked overtime

Dave Mackay (centre) and Roy McFarland leap for a cross as Ian Hutchinson of Chelsea tries to cut out the ball. Derby County versus Chelsea, 12 February 1970.

to get more pennies in. We were still outside playing football as he had his tea and then went out to the pub, so I hardly saw him, but that was typical of those days.

'Dad was Blue – his hero was Dixie Dean – but I was Red, probably because all my mates supported Liverpool, especially the older lads in the street who dictated fashion. My first hero was Billy Liddell, a Scotland international who played centre-forward and outside-left for Liverpool. He was a super player, and after him Bill Shankly bought Ian St John, another favourite of mine, and Ron Yates who played in my position. Ron was colossal, enormous – a god really. It was the time of the Beatles and a great period for the city in terms of the Merseybeat. In our school lunchtimes we used to go down to The Cavern just to open the door and look in. We couldn't afford to go at night.'

After starting in schools football as

Colin Todd and Roy McFarland receive awards before a game against Leeds United in the early 1970s.

an outside-left, Roy was playing in central-midfield by the time he was invited, aged 16, for a trial at Liverpool Boys' Clubs. 'I ended up playing centre-half by accident,' he says. 'After a 20-minute session the whistle went and the coach shouted for the next team to come on. They were short of a centre-half, and I jumped at the opportunity to have a second chance to impress. I played well and they actually chose me to captain the side, a great honour. We played three or four games in Germany on tour and then, back in Liverpool, played Tranmere's youth team at Prenton Park. It was my first experience of playing at a professional ground, and I really enjoyed it. Their centre-forward was Kenny Beamish, who eventually became a teammate. He scored a hat-trick and we lost the game 5–0, but Tranmere noticed me.

'As a trainee accountant I dealt in facts and figures, and I enjoyed the job. When Tranmere came along I had some great support from one of the managers at work who encouraged me to give it a go and reassured me if it didn't work out I could always go back there.'

But number-crunching soon became a distant memory as 35 stylish appearances in the Tranmere back-line during the 1966–67 season alerted the country's top football scouts. The likes of Wolves and Blackpool were apparently interested, as was the only club Roy McFarland really wanted to play for: Bill Shankly's Liverpool.

He had reckoned against the sheer impudence of Derby County's new young manager Brian Clough and sidekick Peter Taylor. After Tranmere had played a Friday night game at the end of August 1967, the pair – who had added McFarland's name to their wish-list while cutting their managerial teeth at Hartlepool – banged on the front door of the McFarland home in Liverpool. It was 1 o'clock in the morning, but they refused to budge until they had captured their man.

Roy's father was instructed to get McFarland junior out of bed and downstairs to sign for the Rams. 'They were both incredibly persuasive,' Roy recalls, 'but it was my father's comment that swung it. He simply said, "If they want you this badly, son, you should sign." They put the forms in front of me, I signed, and they were gone out of the door. They had their first game of the season at Charlton later that day.'

The Derby County revolution was indeed underway, and there was now a tick next to the name of 'McFarland' on Clough and Taylor's list. He cost them £24,000. 'I'd seen Brian Clough on television but to actually meet him in the flesh impressed me more because he was so enthusiastic,' says Roy. 'He

Roy McFarland with the League Championship Trophy, May 1972.

kept telling me he wanted me to be part of the future of Derby County because the club was going to change. To be fair I knew nothing about the club or its history, but Brian made me feel like a giant and convinced me I would play a major part in his revolution. He also told me I would play for England within a year. I had absolutely no idea what he was talking about; I hadn't even considered the possibility of representing my country. But 13 months later I won an Under-23 cap. Brian was out in his forecast by one month.

'Most kids get homesick, and Brian understood this. Initially I was put in a hotel with John O'Hare, who had signed for Derby the week before me, but then he asked Ron Webster, who had just married Doreen, to take me under his wing. Ronnie said yes, and I was really well looked after. Other new teammates like Mick Hopkinson, a full-back who was also a great friend to Kevin Hector, would take me out. Ronnie wasn't a drinker, but Mick would pick me up from the Websters' house in South Normanton on a midweek evening and take me for a drink. Mick didn't last much longer at Derby County, but I'm grateful to people like him for helping me in the early days.'

Roy McFarland and Colin Todd in the mid-1970s.

At the end of his second season with the Rams, the club was heading back to the top tier of English football as Second Division champions and McFarland was voted Player of the Year, a new award in 1969 that demanded the commissioning of a new trophy – the Jack Stamps Trophy – named after the heroic centre-forward of the 1946 FA Cup-winning side. McFarland reckons it is no coincidence that the 1968–69 season was so successful both for the club and for him personally, for it was also Dave Mackay's first campaign in a Derby County shirt.

Discussing the relative merits of Derby's two Championship managers is always a favourite topic for Rams fans, and this is Roy's take on the subject. 'I look at Clough and Taylor as the people who put me in the right direction, but Dave Mackay taught me how to play. I had so many conversations with Brian and Peter about football and life. Brian was interested in how young players developed not only as footballers but as people. In terms of football, though, the guy who taught me everything was Dave.

'We were fortunate at Derby County, as a group of young players coming into that squad in the early days, to have Dave there. He had a tremendous aura, but he wasn't cocky or arrogant with it. He was a down-to-earth guy who would talk to anyone. I lived with him at the Midland Hotel in Derby for a time, and he used to annoy me because other guests wanted to talk to him all the time at the bar

13

Roy McFarland gets up to head Derby's last-minute equaliser against Chelsea at Stamford Bridge in April 1979.

and at dinner, and he would chat while our food got cold. I was happy to talk, within reason, but Dave would give them every minute he had and sign what seemed liked millions of autographs.

'He talked about football, his days at Tottenham, the manager Bill Nicholson, the great players he had played with – Jimmy Greaves, Danny Blanchflower…I got the whole history. On the training ground he was unbelievable – he had a tremendous left foot – but in addition to his ability he supported everyone around the club. He was always accessible. It was only on the football pitch that he played with the arrogance his ability demanded. He knew what he was about.

'When Brian signed him for Derby he was no longer the box-to-box player of old because the engine wasn't there any more, but Brian asked him to sit alongside me and read the game. The reason we had the Second Division Championship success was that Brian also brought Willie Carlin into the side. Willie sat in front of the back four and protected us, especially when Dave needed time out.'

Mackay's influence on defensive partner McFarland undoubtedly helped in persuading Sir Alf Ramsay to give Roy the first of his 28 England caps against Malta in February 1971. After his England debut, more success was around the corner as McFarland skippered the Rams to their first League Championship win in the 1971–72 season.

Halcyon days indeed; and ask Roy to name his toughest opponent on a football pitch and he answers immediately: 'George Best. He was a great player with tremendous skill and great balance. George could head it, score from all angles and tackle like Dave Mackay. Yes, he was the fifth Beatle, the media chased him and we all know what happened. George enjoyed himself off the pitch, but as a footballer he was the best I faced by a mile.'

Ask Roy to name his most talented teammate and it is more of a problem. The man regarded by many as the greatest living ex-Ram frowns for a moment, as if struggling to recall mental images of some of the stars he has played alongside. McFarland's mentor, Mackay, was eventually replaced at Derby by a different type of defender, but one who like his predecessor oozed star quality, when in February 1971 – the month McFarland made his England debut – Brian Clough paid Sunderland £170,000 for Colin Todd. 'Sadly Colin and I didn't play many times together for England because of another great player named Bobby Moore,' Roy says. 'When Colin came to Derby he found it difficult at first because Mackay was playing in the position he wanted to play. He felt uncomfortable at right-back and in midfield, but he knew he would eventually inherit the centre-back berth alongside me. When that happened we immediately understood each other. What helped me was that Colin allowed me to meander up field with the ball and for set-pieces. Colin's instructions from Peter Taylor before every game were simple: "Don't cross the halfway line!"

'Bobby Moore was a legend. It was the back-end of Bobby's international career, so I probably didn't see him at the height of his powers, but as a person he was never flash. He wasn't arrogant, he was down-to-earth; one of the boys. I was lucky to come into an England team with five players who had won the World Cup. I had Gordon Banks behind me, Bobby alongside me, Alan Ball and Martin Peters in front of me and Geoff Hurst in attack. Martin Peters was one of those players you didn't fully appreciate until you had him in your team. I felt, like many other people in football, that the 1970 squad was even better than the squad of '66 – that's why the 1970 World Cup was so disappointing.

'When it comes to favourite teammates I have to mention Kevin Hector. When we were winning things at Derby County in the 1970s it tended to be Toddy and myself who won the media plaudits, while Kevin was the hero of the fans. When I look back now at old videos, the thing I

Arthur Cox and Roy McFarland sign new contracts in 1987.

really notice is the quality of Kevin's finishing. He was unlucky in getting only two England caps. We had some very good players in the England squad, but he deserved better than that.

'But, to answer your question, while Toddy was good and Gordon Banks was probably even better than Peter Shilton, Dave Mackay was the best. You had to play alongside Dave to realise just how great a player he was. Toddy was a different type of player. No one could outrun Colin and he was strong as an ox. He was never renowned for his forward play, but Colin could pass the ball long and short and was underrated in this part of his game. He would always be there as cover, and when I pushed forward a holding midfielder such as John McGovern or Terry Hennessey would automatically drop back alongside him. It worked well.'

It led, I venture, to Roy scoring more than 40 goals for the Rams. 'Forty-nine actually,' he snaps back with a laugh. 'I enjoyed that side of the game. Brian wanted us to play football and get the ball in the box, so it made sense sometimes for me to get up field. We had one of the best crossers of a ball in Alan Hinton. He could hit me from any angle, so sometimes I loitered around at the back post and Alan would invariably deliver the ball where I wanted it.'

When Derby County stunned the football world by winning the League title in 1972, the future seemed rosy indeed for the most stylish England centre-half of his generation, but heartache in an England shirt was followed by a serious injury on international duty, restricting Roy's caps to 28. 'We were preparing for the World Cup qualifier at Wembley against Poland when Alan Ball told me Brian Clough had resigned as manager at Derby,' says Roy. 'It was hard to take in. Before a game we had to win to make the 1974 World Cup finals, I walked out onto the pitch and Brian, who was working for TV that night, appeared and said, "Good luck tonight – don't worry about what has happened, just make sure you win." We were drawing 1–1 and Kevin came on and almost won it late on, but we went out. Those two things in the same week – going out of the World Cup and Brian resigning – must still rate as my lowest moment in football.'

In terms of his playing career, worse was to follow. Also at Wembley, in May 1974, Roy severed an Achilles tendon, an injury that kept him out of all but the last four games of the Rams' second Championship triumph in 1974–75. 'I was playing against Ireland, a rare game alongside Toddy in fact, and I jumped for a ball and something snapped. I didn't realise at first the severity of the injury. It was a Dr Tricky – I'll never forget his name – who told me I'd be out for at least six months. I didn't believe him, though actually it took nine months for me to return to fitness. Unfortunately, while I was out I put too much pressure on my other Achilles and had a partial tear that Dr Tricky also had to repair. Ironically I haven't had any problems since. Dr Tricky did a good job, but I knew I'd lost half a yard of pace, and when I returned I needed Toddy more then than he needed me. It was a difficult time because although I got back into the England team I knew deep inside I wasn't the same player.'

In a season out of the game Roy had an opportunity to reflect on the respective merits of two Championship-winning Rams teams. 'Brian's team was probably more solid than Dave Mackay's; less likely to concede goals, and in Kevin [Hector] we had a guy who could pull something out from any angle and in Alan Hinton a great provider who could also score goals. Dave's side had more flair and, thanks to Bruce Rioch, scored more goals from midfield. In Charlie George after the second Championship season we had another player who should have been chosen more times for England. I played in the only game he played – against the Republic of Ireland – and I know how he felt about being asked to play out of position and then being substituted.

Roy McFarland presents Lee Carsley with the Young Player of the Year award at the Baseball Ground in May 1993.

'Brian's team was more methodical. You knew what you were going to get. Dave's team had something a little bit different thanks to the likes of Bruce, Charlie and Franny Lee. Dave wouldn't mind winning games 5–4, whereas Brian would prefer to win 1–0 or 2–1. That sums them up.'

Though increasingly blighted by injuries, Roy played on at the Baseball Ground through the demise of Mackay and the dark days of Colin Murphy and Tommy Docherty to record more first-team appearances than any other Rams star other than Kevin Hector and his first landlord, Ron Webster.

As player-manager at Bradford City from 1981 he made an immediate impact, winning promotion for the West Yorkshire outfit, and admits he now he should have resisted the lure of his former club when Peter Taylor asked him to team up as assistant manager at Derby in 1983. 'You make decisions in your life, and you have to get on with it. That's what I've done,' says Roy. 'However, I should have stayed longer at Bradford City. They deserved more of my time, and I needed that time in respect of my managerial career. We had been promoted, things were going well – we'd just drawn with Manchester United in the League Cup and were going up to Old Trafford for the replay. I had created something good at Bradford and still needed to learn my trade, but the lure of going back to Derby County was too much. I knew the problems, but I couldn't help myself. Who could resist going back to Derby County? In retrospect, it didn't work out. The club was in decline, and there were problems

17

financially.'

Roy continued to turn out for the first team until finally hanging up his boots in December 1983 and was disappointed not to be interviewed for the manager's job when Taylor left. 'However, I got the call that Arthur Cox wanted to meet me, and he invited me to continue to be part of Derby County,' says Roy. 'Again, in retrospect, despite the lovely times, I probably spent too many years as a number two. Arthur was a very good manager and I learned a hell of a lot from him, but in terms of my career 10 years as a number two was too long, and I should have gone somewhere else. But it was comfortable – Derby County was the club I loved and my family were here.'

The chance to finally take over the hot seat at the Baseball Ground was a long time coming. Lionel Pickering's millions had been spent, the club was back in the second tier…and back in financial trouble. 'A lot of people don't know that my first remit from Lionel as manager was to get £6 million back, so that's what I tried to do,' says Roy. 'That meant selling good players. When we lost in the Play-off Final to Leicester I knew it was going to get increasingly difficult. My days were numbered, and in the last home game of the following season I think all the supporters knew my time was up.'

After leaving Derby in 1995, the managerial merry-go-round took Roy to Bolton, Cambridge United, Torquay United and to Carling Cup heroics with Derbyshire neighbours Chesterfield. But, for this Liverpool lad, Derby has become home. 'Football has changed dramatically both on and off the field during my years in the game,' he says. 'Look at Pride Park Stadium – I had the privilege of playing for two and a half minutes at Ted McMinn's testimonial game. I'd pulled my calf about three days before, but I was determined to get out there one more time. As I hobbled into position Mark Wright told me not to move. I told him not to worry – I couldn't! That was a great experience, and I was quite impressed with Igor [Stimac] – what a nice guy!'

When Roy McFarland made his England debut as a 22-year-old in February 1971, Sir Alf Ramsay wasn't alone in football in believing that this was a player who would be a fixture in the national side for the next decade. The crippling Achilles injury, however, meant things didn't work out that way. Add to this the emotional attachment to Derby County that blurred his thinking during early managerial days and surely Roy must wake up some mornings and want to turn back the clock? 'No. I don't regret anything,' he says unequivocally. 'I don't regret the fact I left Bradford, because it happened. Whatever you do in life, see it through. Football has been part of my life for over 40 years. I signed for Tranmere Rovers the year England won the World Cup and it's been a roller coaster ride.

'To be honest, it's a pleasure to have the chance to talk about the old times because I don't often get asked – it's nice to know perhaps people still want to hear stories about Derby County's glory days. 'As for my particular story – I wouldn't change a thing.'

1969–70 **John O'Hare**

John O'Hare saw it all at close quarters as the story of one of football's greatest managers unfolded. From Brian Clough's earliest days on the training pitches at Sunderland, through Championship glory at Derby, player power at Leeds United to unbelievable European triumphs at Forest, he was there. Energised by Clough's personality, O'Hare lived the dream, shared the good times and sat uncomfortably in player meetings at Elland Road as Bremner, Giles and co. plotted Old Big 'Ead's downfall. John was Clough's first signing as Rams manager, and he didn't need anyone to sell Derby County to him. He was already sold on Clough.

Born in Renton, Dumbartonshire, in 1946, John was spotted playing youth football by Sunderland chief scout Charlie Ferguson. 'From the age of 13 I had an inkling I would be going to Sunderland,' John tells me. 'The first game I ever saw was a local derby between Sunderland and Newcastle and the atmosphere at Roker Park was absolutely electric.'

Number-nine for the Black Cats at that time was the prolific Clough, but when he tore a cruciate ligament on Boxing Day 1962 his career was effectively over. To keep him occupied as he awaited an insurance pay-out, Clough was asked to work with the youth team. 'As a player he was a loner who didn't mix,' says John. 'As a coach he was a different person altogether. He revolutionised training, which in those days consisted of running, running and more running. He introduced a lot of agility work and ball work and made training a pleasure. So we had a strange situation at Sunderland where the first-team players ran around their pitch looking enviously at the young lads who were doing something completely different and altogether more enjoyable.'

While Clough moved on to cut his managerial teeth with sidekick Peter Taylor at Hartlepool, O'Hare broke through at Sunderland, scoring 14 times in 51 appearances. Then, in the summer of 1967, he became available for transfer after falling out with manager Ian McColl. 'Believe it or not, I was a headstrong youth!' says the affable O'Hare. 'I wasn't getting a chance with the likes of Neil Martin and Colin Suggett coming through, so I made my feelings known in a local newspaper. It was a clash of personalities, and McColl put me on the transfer list.'

Clough and Taylor had breezed into Derby keen to make an impact. A paltry £20,000 for a 20-year-old player who was to become arguably the best target man in Derby County's history

John O'Hare.

Manchester United's 18-year-old newcomer Tommy O'Neil just beats Rams player John O'Hare to the ball. Derby County versus Manchester United, 16 August 1971.

John O'Hare and Kevin Hector.

O'Hare goes for goal.

was excellent business. 'They came up to see me, and it was obvious they were different and destined to be successful,' says John. 'I knew absolutely nothing about Derby, but Clough forecast – accurately as it turned out – that Derby on the way up would pass Sunderland on the way down.'

John's first drive to the Baseball Ground is etched in his memory. 'Siddalls Road in those days was yellow because of the fall-out from a local factory, and my first view of the old ground wasn't particularly impressive – it was obliterated by the smoke belching from the Leys Foundry!'

Roy McFarland and Alan Hinton also became new boys at Derby that summer as John made a goalscoring debut against Charlton at the Baseball Ground. A fact that is perhaps overlooked, even by Rams aficionados, is that the Scot introduced by Clough as his new target man, a foil for goal-getter Kevin Hector, had never actually played as a target man in his life! 'As a kid and at Sunderland I played the old-style right-half or inside-left. It was Clough who converted me to centre-forward,' says John.

Ask teammates what John O'Hare ('Solly' to them) was like as a player and they will wax lyrical about his ball control and ability to bring others into the game. It was easy from the stands to underestimate his contribution because, unlike the exciting Hector, he had no great pace. 'I was basically pivotal,' says John. 'Everything was laid up to me and that meant I had to be tough and aware. Kevin on the other hand was a spectacular, eye-catching player with pace – a balanced and graceful runner.'

Ask John to name a similar player in recent times and he has to think hard. 'Playing one-up is fashionable again, but Mark Hughes was probably the last target man who reminded me a bit of myself,' he says, 'though my goals weren't as spectacular!'

John puts his unerring control down to the hours he spent as a nipper, simply knocking a ball against a wall. 'I always had a ball at my feet and I do wonder sometimes today if youth football is too organised,' he says. 'We played in the streets and played for fun. Kids play organised matches these days and the stakes are too high, with too much emphasis placed on winning. I watch my grandson play occasionally and wince at the antics of parents who get too involved.'

While Clough talked hard in his first season in charge at the Baseball Ground, results were not particularly impressive. 'There were glimpses of potential,' says John, 'but it was the following summer with the arrival of Dave Mackay and then Willie Carlin that things really started to happen. Both were experienced, could look after themselves and gave us belief. Dave of course was a legend – a massive influence on the younger players. I remember him turning up for training for the first time at Sinfin Lane. We were all in awe of him and couldn't quite believe Brian Clough had managed to get him to sign for Derby.'

Promotion followed, and Rams fans picked John as their Player of the Year in that first season of consolidation in the top flight. 'We were getting better as a team every season, and eventually we realised we were good enough to win the League,' he says.

The Championship came in 1971–72 when favourite games included a home victory over Leeds and the last one, a must-win at the Baseball Ground against Liverpool. 'The tension that night was incredible, but John McGovern scored the only goal and of course we learned we were champions out in Majorca.'

In five seasons with the Rams, John missed only four games, an incredible feat considering the

John O'Hare receives a pre-match award at the Baseball Ground.

punishment doled out by centre-halves of the day, bruising giants such as Larry Lloyd, Ian Ure, Denis Smith and Jack Charlton. Every team had one.

Season 1972–73 saw the emergence of young striker Roger Davies, and John was occasionally asked to revert to his former midfield role. Clough and Taylor sensationally quit the Baseball Ground in October 1973, and someone at Leeds had the bright idea of replacing England-bound Don Revie with sworn enemy Clough. 'It was a personal thing between Clough and Revie,' says John. 'Ironically, both were from Middlesbrough but they couldn't stand each other, and both sets of players knew it.'

Clough needed friends at Elland Road and went back to Derby to sign O'Hare, who scored 81 goals in 305 games for the Rams, and John McGovern. 'I still have no regrets about going there,' John tells me. 'To be absolutely honest Leeds were a consistently great team in the early 1970s and should have won more trophies. I really enjoyed beating them as a Derby player, but you had to admire the quality of their team. Remember too that Billy Bremner, Eddie Gray and Peter Lorimer were all Scotland teammates, so there was no animosity towards me, they just didn't like Brian or his methods, especially as he seemed to want to change things too quickly.

'I knew he wasn't going to last long because even the new signings – John McGovern, Duncan McKenzie and me – were invited to meetings called by the players. There was no secrecy. It was soon clear player power would get Clough out.'

Clough famously lasted just 44 days before being replaced by Jimmy Armfield. 'Jimmy was a real gentleman who understood my situation,' says John. 'I had originally intended to move house to Leeds but sensibly had second thoughts and stayed put in Ockbrook. When Brian took over at Forest I joined

The goal that clinched the League Championship. Liverpool's Tommy Smith watches John McGovern's winner on its way into the net at the Baseball Ground in May 1972. John O'Hare is the other Rams player.

John O'Hare and Alan Durban hold aloft the League Championship trophy at the Baseball Ground in 1972.

him again, mainly because it was convenient. I knew, of course, he would improve things at Forest, but I never imagined he would take them to such heights, especially in the early days. Actually, it wasn't until Peter Taylor rejoined him that he recaptured his enthusiasm and built a Forest team that was an identikit of his best side at Derby.'

In recent years John has scouted for Martin O'Neill, a teammate from Forest's European adventures. 'I've worked for Martin since his Leicester days, and while he's not quite so abrasive and arrogant as Brian used to be, there are similarities between the two, particularly in the way Martin deals with players,' says John. 'When he was at Celtic I used to do all his reports on Champions League opponents, which was great, but I'm happy just getting out and watching football.

'My wife is from Durham, and it was always our intention to eventually move back to the North East, but Derby is really convenient for my job, which takes me all over the country. The family have grown up here, the people are friendly and it's a nice easy-going city. I just like the place.'

1970–71 **Dave Mackay**

It says something about the astonishing aura of one of the true legends of British football when you discover he actually stands only 5ft 9in tall. On a football pitch, for anyone fortunate enough to have seen him in action, Dave Mackay was a giant.

Miscast by many observers, especially during his Derby days, as one of football's hard men, Mackay was in fact an incredibly skilful player, renowned for the sweetness of his left foot. His party trick in his prime was to flick an old penny coin from his foot onto his forehead and jiggle it down into his eye. 'We wore suede shoes in those days and that helped!' he tells me.

Dave is also happy to confirm as accurate the account in Alan Mullery's autobiography of Tottenham assistant manager Eddie Bailey describing at a training session the near impossible trick of being able to volley a football against a wall continuously, using alternate feet, without the ball ever hitting the floor. Mackay stepped forward, took the ball from Bailey, and announced: 'Do you mean something like this?' before treating his teammates to a master class in the trick Bailey had described.

It was pure Mackay. As was the intimidating habit of leading his side out onto the pitch, kicking the ball high into the air before trapping it with unerring control.

So it matters little that the picture on the wall of the front room at Dave's home in the village of Burton Joyce, Nottinghamshire, commemorates his achievements as a double-winner with Tottenham. It matters still less that he regards his greatest achievement in the game as winning the Scottish Championship with his beloved Hearts.

Dave Mackay signs an autograph in 1969.

To Rams fans, Dave Mackay is the barrel-chested leader who organised, scolded and cajoled a young Derby side to the Second Division title in 1969 and then helped to consolidate the club's position in the top flight ahead of a memorable first Championship title, before returning as manager to guide the Rams to a second First Division triumph in 1975.

Natural talent is one thing, but ability has to be nurtured, and it was during the war years in his native Edinburgh that Dave honed his football skills. 'I had three brothers, two of whom also signed for Hearts, so we were a family of good footballers,' says Dave. 'We were born next to Carrick Knowe Golf Course which had a railway bridge, and you could volley a ball against a brick wall there. We used a tennis ball, and the wall wasn't flat so would come back at awkward angles.'

Dave's Tottenham training ground heroics

Derby County captain Dave Mackay holds the trophy high. The Rams are Division Two champions in 1969.

are thus explained. 'I had brothers who, like me, always wanted to play football, but even if you were on your own you could use a tennis ball against that wall – right foot, left foot, practising your volleying. It was always football. Even on the way to school we would run along the pavement dribbling a tennis ball.'

The young Mackay had only two ambitions in life. One was to play for Hearts; the other to play for his country. As a fan he had cheered on his club's 'Terrible Trio' of Conn, Bauld and Wardhaugh and was thrilled to eventually play alongside them and another Hearts legend John Cumming. 'My finest moment in football was winning the League in 1957 with Hearts,' he says. 'I will never forget being at the corner of the ground near Gorgie Road and hoisting the flag as captain. I was Hearts crazy, as were the whole family.'

By the age of 22 Dave had also made his Scotland debut against Spain at the Bernabeu. To say Mackay was a reluctant recruit to the English game at the end of the 1958–59 campaign is understating the case. 'It was a shock when Tottenham came in, and I really didn't want to go,' explains Dave. 'My mum told me Bill Nicholson was coming up to see me. By that time I'd broken my foot three times diving into tackles, and I think the Hearts directors were keen to take the cash because they probably thought if I did it again I would be finished. A £30,000 transfer in those days was big money. So I was sick at the time, but it was probably the best move I ever made.'

Two years after signing for a struggling Spurs, Bill Nicholson's side became only the second English club to do 'the double' – winning the League and FA Cup. 'There were some great players down there,' says Dave, 'and doing the double was absolutely fantastic. We started so well in the League that season and it seemed to come easily. No one gave us any problems, and the likes of Cliff Jones, Danny Blanchflower and Terry Dyson were all smashing players. Of course I always say it's the three Scots Bill Nick brought in – John White, Bill Brown and yours truly – who made the difference!'

Another FA Cup triumph followed in 1962 and then a third, with Mackay as skipper, in 1967. In between, the box-to-box midfielder missed 16 months of football when he broke his left leg in a tussle with Manchester United's Noel Cantwell at Old Trafford. 'The first break was a big foul so far as I was concerned,' says Dave. 'I went to shoot the ball and Cantwell's boot came in and mangled my leg. My fibula and tibia were both smashed to the extent that my left toe came up to my left knee. When I sat up I was frightened to take off the tie-up on my sock, because it seemed to be the only thing holding my leg together.'

Celebrating promotion, 1969.

A diabolical late tackle in his comeback game against Shrewsbury reserves a year later meant more hard work for Mackay. 'I would spend hours running up and down the terracing, but I was determined to get back,' he says. 'Now I have one straight leg and one bandy leg. As a kid they used to say all footballers had bandy legs, and I remember trying to walk like that – now I can half do it for real!'

The pain and frustration of his time on the sidelines explains the famous image of

Dave Mackay taking charge at Derby in 1973.

him lifting Leeds United's ferocious Scottish midfielder Billy Bremner off the ground by his shirt with a single flex of the Mackay bicep. 'It was during my comeback after the second break,' he says. 'There was a throw-in down the line and I pushed Billy over. We were always battling. He got up, came past my right leg and then whacked me on my left leg. He didn't break it, thankfully, because that would have been it for me, but I was so angry I grabbed him. At that moment I could have lifted an elephant!

'Actually, we were mates off the pitch – he was a good lad – and I didn't hit him or anything! I just picked him up because he was smaller than me. Leeds were a dirty team and these sort of things happened. There were certain players you just couldn't allow to mess with you.'

Misinformed pundits have described Dave, at certain football functions, as a hard man – even dirty. Mackay scowls at the description. 'Yes, so dirty I never got sent off in my life!' he tells me.

At the end of the 1967–68 season, Hearts was beckoning again for Dave, who had decided his Tottenham days were over. The Tynecastle side fancied the legendary Mackay, now 33, as player-manager. 'I'd done quite well in that last season at White Hart Lane,' says Dave, 'but then Malcolm Allison's Manchester City came down to us, and for the first time in my time at Tottenham we were outplayed on our pitch. The following Monday I went to see Bill Nick and said I couldn't do the job of getting up and down the pitch any longer. Bill agreed to let me go, and although Hearts wanted me I didn't want to fail at Tynecastle. I had hero status there and didn't want the fans turning on me because I was a shadow of what I had once been. So I went to Derby because, to be brutally honest, the idea of failing there didn't seem nearly as bad as failing in my home town.

'I didn't know much about Brian Clough, but he told me, "David, if you come to Derby County we will win the Second Division." So I signed – but when I checked the papers and saw where Derby had finished the previous season, just above the relegation zone, I really thought I'd made a massive mistake. I knew I was getting fatter, putting on weight, but Brian didn't worry. He gave me a new role as sweeper alongside a young lad called Roy McFarland and simply told me to lead the team.

'In the past I'd had enough energy to run up and down the pitch all day, but that had gone, so playing sweeper was great for me. I was the boss. I would yell at the likes of Roy, Colin Todd, Archie Gemmill and Ronnie Webster to pick up people – it was a piece of cake! I honestly thought I could still be playing in that position when I was 50. It was the easiest season of my life, but of course then we won promotion and it got tough again.'

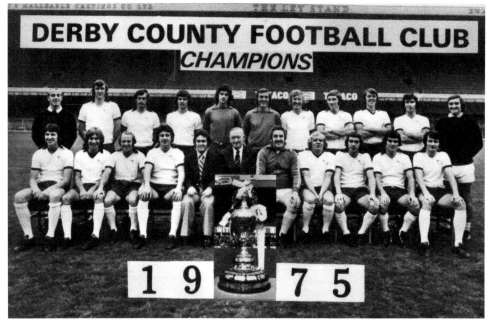

Derby County, Football League champions 1974–75. Chairman Sam Longson sits between manager Dave Mackay and secretary Stuart Webb.

At the end of his first season with the Rams, Dave Mackay was joint Footballer of the Year with Manchester City's Tony Book, and back in the top flight the Derby skipper was to enjoy more success, not least in the 5–0 Baseball Ground mauling of Bill Nicholson's Spurs.

While Brian Clough was always quick to describe 'David Mackay' as the catalyst for what he went on to achieve in football management, Mackay himself was happy simply to be the boss on the pitch and an inspiration for Derby's talented squad on the training ground.

'I always mention Peter Taylor in the same breath as Brian because I thought they were brilliant together and not so good apart,' says Dave. 'They had this happy knack of signing the right players and Brian, despite his reputation, never crossed me. He used to give me Mondays and Tuesdays off because I lived in London, and even when we got beaten on a Saturday he'd tell everyone in the dressing room, in that way of his, not to be late on Monday and then, as an aside, say to me, "I'll see you on Wednesday David".'

I well recall the look of bemusement on Dave Mackay's face at a Pride Park fans' forum in 2002 when he shared a platform with the late great Clough. Dave, microphone in hand, was asked a direct question from the floor. Before he had time even to open his mouth, Cloughie answered it for him.

Everyone laughed, including Dave. The legendary Mackay hardly got a word in edgeways that night as Clough bossed the event and had happy Rams fans cheering for more. Yes, Old Big 'Ead always had to have the last word and, while the first Championship-winning manager in Derby County's history had the utmost respect for the manager who led the club to its second title, the name of Brian Clough came to haunt Dave's time in the hot seat at the Baseball Ground.

Clough's powers of persuasion had worked superbly well in bringing Mackay to the Baseball Ground for a thrilling finale to his playing days after glorious years with Hearts and Tottenham. Clough credited

Mackay – a year his senior – with managing his young Derby County side on the field of play. But Clough could be ruthless. After helping the Rams to the old Second Division title in his first season and enjoying two seasons (fourth and ninth) back in the top flight, Mackay was off-loaded after the arrival of record signing Colin Todd. He signed off with a 100 per cent League appearance record (as did, incidentally, John O'Hare and Kevin Hector that season), and was voted Player of the Year. 'I found the First Division fairly hard second time around but still coped with it,' Dave tells me. 'I probably would have stayed, but Peter and Brian were no mugs. They could see I was at the end of the road, so they sold me to Swindon. Not only that, they actually made a profit on me at 37 years old!'

That was in May 1971. By the end of the year Mackay had stepped up to become player-manager at Swindon and in November 1972 was appointed boss at Nottingham Forest. Eleven months later, in October 1973, the call came again from the Baseball Ground after Clough and Taylor sensationally walked out on Derby County. 'If I'd still been playing at Derby I would have been one of the most vocal guys demanding the reinstatement of Brian Clough,' Dave says. 'I would have fought to try and keep him. Luckily I knew the players, and that was crucial because anyone coming in who didn't know them wouldn't have stood a chance.

'Roy McFarland was a big pal of mine, as were one or two others, so I didn't have much of a problem. The papers played it up at the time. I used to get calls from journalists claiming certain players would be protesting about Brian's departure by not turning up for training, but that never happened. I knew the ones who might be a bit of a problem, so I sorted them out.'

Still, it took Mackay and his assistant Des Anderson eight games to record their first win, just before Christmas 1973, with goals from Roger Davies and Alan Hinton in a 2–0 victory at Newcastle. The signing of Bruce Rioch for £200,000 from Aston Villa in February 1974 was a masterstroke which led to a third-place finish in the First Division, guaranteeing the Rams a UEFA Cup spot. Better was to come.

Manager Dave Mackay and the Rams team with the League Championship at the Baseball Ground on 26 April 1975, before the final game of the season against Carlisle United. Afterwards the infamous Baseball Ground pitch was dug up.

Mackay returns to the scene of former glories – the last League game at the Baseball Ground in May 1997.

Despite an Achilles injury picked up on England duty keeping Roy McFarland out for most of the 1974–75 campaign, the Rams, skippered by Archie Gemmill, were set to record their second League title in three years. The capture of 30-year-old Francis Lee from Manchester City in August 1974 was inspired. 'Franny is what I call a real man,' says Dave. 'I knew players like him wouldn't stand for any crap.'

Rioch's contribution from midfield was phenomenal, ending the season with 15 goals. 'Bruce was one of the first players who would shoot from 30 yards and regularly score goals,' says Dave. 'He had so much power – thighs like tree trunks!'

The Rams, with Player of the Year Peter Daniel filling in for the injured McFarland, lifted the title with a two-point advantage over Liverpool and Ipswich. Mackay was satisfied. 'I expected to win every time I played, and the same went for the teams I managed. Realistically, though, I would have taken a top four place that season, so the title was a nice bonus.'

In the summer of 1975 Mackay strengthened his side again, bringing in Arsenal's supremely talented Charlie George for a bargain £100,000. 'Charlie was a brilliant signing; I knew him from my Tottenham days. I was in Edinburgh taking a break when Des Anderson called me to say Charlie was about to sign for Tottenham. I told Des to tell Charlie we wanted him at the Baseball Ground.'

Charlie's 24 goals in season 1975–76 included a hat-trick in the 4–1 Baseball Ground victory over mighty Real Madrid in the European Cup second round in October. 'You will never get another night like that one,' he says. 'A 1–0 win would have been great, but we slaughtered them. That night was unbelievable and must rate as one of Derby's greatest results ever.'

Mackay's Rams were flying so high that season that another record signing, Leighton James, brought in from Burnley in November, couldn't get anywhere near the first team for a month. When Charlie George dislocated a shoulder playing against Stoke City in March 1976, Derby County were chasing a possible League and FA Cup double, but slumped to a relatively disappointing fourth position in Division One and a semi-final Cup exit against Manchester United at Hillsborough.

'Charlie getting injured made a big difference to that season,' Dave concedes. 'Semi-finals are always difficult games because even the best teams let nerves get the better of them. I never lost a Final, even as a schoolboy, so not getting to Wembley with Derby was hard.'

Even after an astounding return of third, first and fourth positions in English football's top flight, Dave Mackay was not safe in his job. Throughout his time in the Baseball Ground hot seat the name of Brian Clough was always in the background. A poor start to the 1976–77 campaign and the knives were out. Eight games without a win was followed by the 8–2 home thrashing of Tottenham. Rioch, playing as an emergency striker, scored four and George three, but it wasn't enough to save Dave. 'I kept getting reports that the board wanted Brian back. I read in one of the papers that three or four of the board had been on the golf course talking about this, so I went into the boardroom and had a right go,' says Dave. 'I more or less told them to get stuffed.

'Then I returned to my office and had second thoughts; after all, I had a mortgage to pay. I went back and told them I'd changed my mind, but they hadn't changed theirs. I was annoyed that even after everything I'd achieved for Derby County the board still wanted to bring back Brian. Of course, Brian never did come back, but that was me gone.'

Dave eventually left the country and enjoyed almost a decade managing the best teams in Kuwait and Dubai, 'making a few quid' along the way. Now, at his home in Burton Joyce, he reflects on his most difficult opponents in football. One is English; the other a Scot. 'They were both inside-forwards I came up against while playing as a midfield wing-half,' Dave says. 'Johnny Haynes of Fulham and England was a bogey man for me, not least when he played in the England team that beat Scotland 9–3. The only saving grace is that I scored for Scotland, so it could have been worse! The other has to be Denis Law of Manchester United and Scotland. A brilliant player.'

As for the most talented individual he ever played alongside, Dave goes for Jimmy Greaves. 'Jimmy was a natural footballer who could do anything,' he says. 'Kevin Hector was the same type of player. Both had natural ability and were brilliant goalscorers. Neither were particularly good trainers, but on the park they did what they were supposed to do – score goals. They didn't have to work too hard at it, and any manager who tried to force them to train harder was a fool. The best way was to let them do their own thing.'

For a moment his mind goes back to one match that for many Rams fans signalled the start of the glory days – a League Cup replay against Chelsea on the night of 2 October 1968 in front of 34,346 fans at the Baseball Ground.

'Ah yes, the 3–1 win against Chelsea,' he grins. 'They had Peter Osgood, Chopper Harris – all the big names – and we beat them 3–1. I scored. There was nothing quite like the atmosphere of a night match at the Baseball Ground.'

1971–72 **Colin Todd**

I still recall the moment I knew Colin Todd was the most exciting defender I would ever see.

In 1972 I was a grace-and-favour supporter reliant on the possibility of being allowed the use of an uncle's spare season ticket. Luckily, in the December of that year, I was treated to the big pre-Christmas match at the Baseball Ground. The Rams were the reigning League champions, Toddy was the club's reigning Player of the Year and just short of 29,000 were crammed into the old stadium.

The opponents that day were Newcastle United, whose muscular and side-burned centre-forward was, to this 11-year-old *Shoot* magazine subscriber, simply a beast. The fastest striker bar none, Malcolm Macdonald bounced central-defenders for fun before skipping away from them in a furious bow-legged gallop.

Newcastle's defenders, organised by the clever Bobby Moncur, had little use for their midfield players. They simply lumped the ball over the top for 'Supermac', who would glare at the line of defenders alongside him on the halfway line before setting off, winning the race and scoring the goal. Simple. Macdonald was out of the blocks as fast as an Olympic sprinter and the defenders were

Colin Todd receives the PFA Player of the Year trophy in 1975.

nowhere. I remember him taking part in the popular *Superstars* TV programme at the time and blitzing his sporting opponents out of sight in the 100m event in 10.4 seconds, on a cinder track with heavy spikes. At the time that made him the third-fastest sprinter in the UK and could have won him a place on the 4x100m relay team for the Montreal Olympics. He was *that* fast.

I knew, of course, that McFarland and Todd were good defenders, but every time Macdonald received a pass that afternoon I fully expected him to score. I need not have worried. McFarland, returning after a two-match suspension had the striker in his pocket and, in any case, even when Derby's captain attacked the first ball, there was always Todd backing him up.

Then came the moment I had dreaded, the through ball SuperMac had been waiting for. The striker was onto it in a flash and the Rams' two central-defenders were caught square on the halfway line as the Newcastle man scampered off towards Colin Boulton's goal. Todd gave chase, and to my

Colin Todd and Henry Newton with the League Championship trophy in 1975.

astonishment he miraculously caught the speed merchant on the edge of the Derby box. Not only that, he neatly nicked the ball away from Macdonald's lethal left peg before running the ball upfield again, passing a relieved McFarland on the way. SuperMac simply stood on the edge of the Derby box, hands on hips, a beaten man.

When Toddy arrived at Pride Park Stadium as Jim Smith's new assistant in November 2000 it was my great pleasure to interview the great man. I immediately reminded him of that tremendous tackle against Newcastle 28 years before and ventured: 'You were incredibly quick weren't you?' He frowned a little, considering his response, before replying in his North-Eastern brogue: 'Aye, but I could play a bit as well you know.'

He was right to challenge my shallow observation. Not only was Todd scintillatingly fast, he was strong, read the game brilliantly and passed the ball crisply, usually to a teammate in a more advantageous position.

Defenders are appreciated, but they are not exciting. Goalscorers are exciting, mazy wingers are exciting, probing midfielders are exciting, but not defenders. But Todd was. I can still see him now in my mind's eye, his thick blond hair bouncing in time to his stride as he brought the ball out of defence after another crucial interception, and I can hear the appreciative applause that used to cascade around every part of the Baseball

Ground – a gesture afforded only to very special players. A teammate in later years, Charlie George, used to draw the same reaction when he effortlessly changed the direction of play with an inch-perfect 40–yard pass. Players had to be recognised as special to win that sort of crowd approval.

Born into a mining family in Chester-le-Street and a Newcastle fan as a boy, Todd chose Roker Park and not St James' Park when his blossoming talent attracted the big local clubs. 'It was the red-and-whites I chose because of their tradition for youth,' he says, and it was at Sunderland that Todd met a man who would shape his career – Brian Clough, then youth-team coach.

Moving on to Hartlepool before taking over the hot seat at Derby, Clough monitored Todd's progress as the youngster played 173 League games for the Black Cats from 1966.

With the town of Derby reeling after the shock financial collapse of its major employer Rolls-Royce in February 1971, Clough made his move, paying a record £170,000 to bring his protégé to the Baseball Ground. If there seemed something overtly decadent about paying that kind of money for a mere footballer at such a devastating time for Derby's workers, it was soon forgotten as Todd proved himself to be anything but a 'mere' footballer.

He joined a side doing pretty well in their second top-flight campaign under Clough. The Rams were beating the middling teams such as Nottingham Forest, who had been despatched 4–2 at the City Ground in November 1970 with goals from McGovern, O'Hare, Wignall and Gemmill. But the ambitious Clough wanted more; he wanted to compete with the best teams in the country.

With captain Dave Mackay well into his groove in an ever-present last season as a player at the Baseball Ground, Todd was picked in midfield for his debut at home against Arsenal on 27

Controlling the ball with typical poise.

Colin Todd, soon to be Derby County assistant manager, 21 October 2000.

Colin Todd at Pride Park stadium for the press conference to announce his appointment as the new manager of Derby County Football Club.

February. League and FA Cup double winners that season, the Gunners were beaten 2–0 with goals from Man of the Match McFarland and Hector. As Mackay saw out the campaign, Todd dutifully played out of position either in midfield or at right full-back, but at the start of the 1971–72 season he was in central-defence, on the way to the first of two League Championship medals and a brilliant partnership with McFarland.

Todd played 40 games in the 1971–72 Championship side, throwing in two rare goals for good measure, one in the 4–0 home trouncing of Stoke City, the other in a Baseball Ground draw against Tottenham. This was to be Derby County's greatest season, and Todd was the Player of the Year.

The legendary Bobby Moore, on his way to 108 caps and still playing for England in 1973, restricted Todd's international appearances to a miserly 27, even while he displayed a remarkable consistency at club level, playing 41 League games in 1972–73, 40 in 1973–74 and 39 in the second Championship season of 1974–75, probably his greatest as a player. Although Peter Daniel, a commendable deputy that campaign for the injured McFarland, won the fans' vote as Player of the Year, it was widely accepted that Todd was 'out of this world'. His fellow professionals certainly thought so, voting him the 1975 PFA Players' Player of the Year.

Todd did not miss a game the following season, and he had made 371 appearances in all competitions for the Rams when Tommy Docherty, seemingly intent on making himself as unpopular as possible with the Derby fans, sold him to Everton for £300,000 in September 1978, still three months short of his 30th birthday. Toddy's time on Merseyside was brief. He moved on to Birmingham City in 1979 before joining up again with Clough at Forest for two seasons from 1982.

As a manager, his clubs have included Middlesbrough, Bolton Wanderers, Swindon Town, Bradford City, and after becoming Jim Smith's assistant in 2000 he was given an astonishingly short period – 15 Premiership matches – in charge at Derby County. In June 2007 he was appointed manager of Danish Superliga side Randers FC.

As a player, however, he was one of Derby's greatest.

1972–73 **Kevin Hector**

Indulge me for a moment, if you will.

Back in the days when PC games such as *Championship Manager* were no more than a futuristic football dream and computers were, in any case, as big as Derby Cathedral, devotion to your favourite Rams player could still be expressed…albeit on the back of a school exercise book.

I blew the dust off one of mine quite recently, a Parwich Junior School English book from 1969, and on the back I'd drawn a diagram charting a passing movement that started with Durban in midfield, progressed to Hinton on the left and saw O'Hare flick it on at the near post for Hector to pounce with the finish.

Who else? Kevin Hector, The King of Derby County, my hero – a sublime striker who not only walked on water, he skated over the Baseball Ground bog into which hapless defenders seemed to sink without trace.

In the school playground I *was* Kevin Hector. Every goal I scored had The King's name on it. Not that he needed any help from me. By the time he finally hung up his Derby County boots in 1982 he had scored 203 goals and pulled on a Rams shirt more times than any player in the club's history.

Almost 40 years on from my schoolboy doodles, we drank pints together in the sunshine outside Kevin's local – the Woodlands in Allestree. Nut-brown from walking the steamy streets of Derby on his post round during the summer months, he was still tipping the scales at his old playing weight despite being old enough to qualify for a bus pass.

He smiled at my exercise book anecdote and mentioned he scribbled similar diagrams during his own schooldays in Leeds, when gentle giant John Charles was his hero. Kevin spoke quietly and philosophically, his sharp green eyes still twinkling with pride when reminded of past glories. Sometimes the memories were so intense, they seemed to water.

Chelsea, League Cup, 1969: 'That match sticks in my mind as probably the greatest game at the Baseball Ground for atmosphere,' Kevin tells me. 'I never heard them make as much noise as that. Normally when you are on the field you cannot really hear the crowd because you are concentrating, but the noise that night was deafening.

'Chelsea took the lead, but then Dave Mackay equalised from a set-piece just before half-time, and that's when it started.

Striker Kevin Hector (right) tries to get away from the challenge of Forest skipper Peter Hindley, 28 November 1970.

Hector takes on the Wolves defence.

Coming out for the second half we knew we were going to win. It was us and the crowd against Chelsea. Alan Durban got the second and I sealed it – an amazing night. In fact it took ages to wind down afterwards – we were all on such a high. I never used to get any sleep after games like that. Incredible.'

Every bit as incredible, in fact, as The King's first experience of the Baseball Ground: September 1966, in an England still bathed in the afterglow of World Cup triumph.

After unsuccessful trials with Hull City and Wolves, young Kevin had signed on for Bradford Park Avenue, managed by Jimmy Scoular, famously described by the late great Duncan Edwards as the finest tackler he had ever seen. As well as being Kevin's first boss, Jimmy was still turning out at right-half and gave his young right-winger a roasting every time he lost the ball. 'I was scared to death of Jimmy,' Kevin recalls, 'and after three or four games he left me out. Then the reserve-team coach decided to try me up front and it just happened – I never stopped scoring.'

Aged just 21 years and 156 days when he found the net for the 100th time in Football League games (only Jimmy Greaves and Dixie Dean achieved the feat at a younger age), Kevin finished the 1965–66 season as the League's top scorer with 44 goals.

So when Tim Ward's Derby County came a-calling at the start of the next campaign, presumably they were ready to roll out the red carpet for this prolific young star in the making? Not a bit of it.

'There were no agents in those days,' says Kevin, his eyes narrowing at the thought. 'My father came down with me on the train from Leeds with our assistant manager Jock Buchanan, who had once played for Derby County. At Derby Station we got a trolley bus to the Baseball Ground and met the manager

Hector celebrates another goal.

Kevin Hector (left), Glenn Skivington and Kevin Wilson (right) in action during the Rams' 1–1 draw with Charlton Athletic at the Baseball Ground in February 1982.

and the board. I was just learning to drive so I didn't have a car. Today new signings are picked up in limousines and even helicopters, but it was different in those days. I remember taking in the Baseball Ground and thinking, "This is some ground!" It was early season, September, so the pitch was nice, and I liked it straight away.'

First impressions from Rams fans about their record signing were mixed. 'They weren't sure what they were getting to start with,' Kevin admits. 'Forty thousand pounds was a lot of money in those days and they perhaps thought the club had signed a big centre-forward; that's what they were used to. When they saw this 5ft 8in skinny striker I think it confused them until they saw I had some pace and frightened defenders. I loved the Baseball Ground from the first game, a 4–1 victory over Huddersfield. I scored, and I even enjoyed the surface, which was actually better than I was used to at Bradford. Hopefully the fans thought they had got something a little bit special.'

For the benefit of younger fans who never saw The King in the flesh, I asked him to nominate 21st century versions of Kevin Hector. 'Today I would say Craig Bellamy, because he likes to take players on, and Jermaine Defoe. Those are the two that spring to mind,' says Kevin. 'I never played 'up top' as an out-and-out striker. I used to venture left and right and come deep. Sometimes I played wide right, but I wouldn't stick to that – I would go looking for the ball, just like Wayne Rooney does today.

'I had a free role, and one good thing about Brian Clough and Dave Mackay when they were my

Hector arrives at Burton Albion's Eton Park.

managers at Derby County is that they gave me freedom to roam. Brian would just say: "Go out and do your stuff!"'

Not that the striker Rams fans soon christened 'The King' was particularly easy in the role of crowd-pleaser. Quiet rather than cocky off the field of play, he needed help in adapting to the demands of a real football city. 'Mick Hopkinson was the first player to take me under his wing,' says Kevin. 'He was a real character, a local lad from Belper, and I suppose he showed me the ropes.'

While Kevin got Rams fans talking, he could not prevent manager Tim Ward losing his job at the end of the 1966–67 season. 'My first memory of Brian Clough is of him coming into the dressing room. He'd already kept us waiting for half an hour, and none of us knew what to expect. Finally he appeared, and the first person he spoke to was one of our older players Reg Matthews, the goalkeeper. Brian glanced down at him and said "Bloody hell Reg, are you still playing?" Then he told Reg to get rid of the cigarette he was smoking. That was it. Those were the first words he spoke. He never had any one-to-one sessions with me. We had team meetings where Brian might pick one or two people out, but nothing specific – that's the way he worked.'

Brian returned to former club Sunderland for his first signing as Derby manager. 'John O'Hare was a great target man – probably one of the best at that time,' says Kevin. 'You could bang a ball up to him in training and in matches and it would just stick. He wouldn't give it away. I don't think fans really appreciated that. They wanted him to turn with the ball and take players on like I did, but his control of the ball and the way he brought other player into the game was invaluable.'

Another mediocre season followed, and Kevin has no doubt about the catalyst for the Rams' change in fortunes. 'It really all stated when Brian signed Dave Mackay,' he tells me. 'Dave was a massive name in football, and to get someone with his ability to come up from London gave the club a lift both on and off the field.'

With Mackay barking instructions from the back, the Rams won the old Second Division Championship with ease, seven points clear of runners up Crystal Palace in the days when a win was worth two points. Derby won every one of their last nine matches, signing off with the 5–0 thrashing of Bristol City at the Baseball Ground, and Hector was top scorer with 20 goals. 'We had a good blend of youth and experience, and we knew Brian would add to the squad,' Kevin recalls. 'And he was ruthless. Willie Carlin had done a great job for us in the promotion season, but Brian replaced him with Archie Gemmill, and that was a great signing.

'Most of my goals came from Alan Hinton. He was a superb winger, not to everyone's tastes, but I knew exactly what he was going to do. He went down that left wing and crossed it in. He didn't mess about. He just beat his man once and got his cross in so I knew which run to make, either near post or back post. He was quicker than he looked too. We had little sprints in training, and over 20 or 30 yards he was quick.'

'But you were quicker?' I ventured.

'Oh yes, I was the quickest in the club; and Toddy was just behind me,' Kevin replies, grinning again.

Respected sports journalist Gerald Mortimer was asked recently to nominate his best Rams players of all time, and he placed Kevin at number three, just behind Roy McFarland and the legendary Steve Bloomer. 'I have no problem with that,' says Kevin. 'Roy was a superb footballer. He could have played at centre-forward just as well as centre-half, and in that way he reminded me of one of my favourite players, John Charles. Roy was perhaps too good a footballer to play at centre-half. That said, he could be nasty too. He certainly kicked us in training!'

I mentioned my first-ever experience of the Baseball Ground: the 4–4 draw with Manchester United on a snowy Boxing Day in 1970. In my naïvety at the time, and amazed to be so close to the likes of Kevin and United legends George Best, Bobby Charlton and Denis Law, I thought all football games were that exciting! Kevin grinned again. 'There's no way these days that match would have been played,' he says. 'The pitch was covered in snow and unfit, but it was Boxing Day, there was a big crowd in and the ref decided we ought to give it a go. Entertainment-wise you certainly got your money's worth!'

At the end of the following season, Derby County were champions of all England. 'The first Championship took us by surprise,' Kevin admits. 'We were on holiday as a squad in Majorca, and I don't think any of us really thought we would win it. Leeds had to get a point at Wolves and lost, and Liverpool had to win, but drew. We celebrated that night, but it really only sank in when we returned to Derby about a week later. We got on a bus, and the roads to the Baseball Ground were heaving with people, and the stadium itself was packed. We all had our blue suits on. I can remember the whole thing like it was yesterday.'

From the day he signed on for Bradford Park Avenue to the day he hung up his boots at the Baseball Ground in 1982, Kevin Hector never had an agent. 'You had to go in and see Brian when your contract was up, and there was no one to fight your battles for you,' he recalls with a grimace. 'Brian ran a tight ship – we were all more or less on the same money. He looked after us in his own way in that he was good on bonuses if we were successful. I wasn't in Derby when Brian resigned, I was on England squad duty with Roy, Toddy and David Nish. We were in a hotel in Hertfordshire and Emlyn Hughes came up and asked us if we'd heard the news. We were sitting together at a table after training and he just came out with it.'

Cloughie had dominated national newspaper headlines the previous week by describing Jan Tomaszewski, the goalkeeper of England's World Cup qualifier opponents Poland, as 'a clown'. England needed to beat Poland at Wembley to progress to the 1974 Finals and Kevin was shocked to be included in Sir Alf Ramsey's squad. 'I thought my England chance had passed me by because I was 29, but suddenly the call came out of the blue. Meeting Bobby Moore and talking to him properly for the first time was a great experience, but the game itself was a disaster. Coming on with two minutes to go and the score 1–1, I remember a corner coming in from the left and the goalkeeper was nowhere. He actually caught me on the back of the head with his hand, but I still connected perfectly with my header. It hit one of their players on the knee at the near post and then bounced out to someone and that effort hit the far post. The lad on the line had absolutely no idea he had stopped my header.

'If that had gone in I would have been at the World Cup in Germany in '74 and would probably have played. People still come up to me and ask me whether I remember that game…and of course I do!'

Back at Derby, the board acted quickly to appoint the only man who could possibly have stepped into Brian Clough's trainers – Dave Mackay. 'Sam Longson was pretty cute after Brian had gone, he didn't mess about and that was that,' says Kevin. 'In the same way Clough had persuaded Dave to come to Derby, we were amazed when Dave, as manager, brought in Franny Lee and then Charlie George. That was some management! Plus he bought Bruce Rioch to add to the players who were already there.

'I enjoyed the first Championship more than the second in 1975, but with Charlie in the team the following season we were really flying, and at one point a League and Cup double was on the cards. Then Charlie got injured just before the semi-final against Manchester United. That game at Hillsborough was probably my biggest disappointment in football. We didn't perform on the day and United were the better side.'

FA Cup semi-final defeat signalled the start of a dramatic slide in fortunes for the Rams, precipitating the departure of Mackay and the eventual arrival of an ex-United boss known as 'The Doc'. 'Tommy Docherty came in and started changing everything, getting rid of players. That's when it started falling to pieces,' says Kevin. 'He told me straight away that he was going to bring his own players in and I would be leaving. All I could say was "Fair enough". But he ruined the team. He brought players in who weren't good enough and let his best players go.'

Ten years after signing on for the Rams, Kevin Hector joined Vancouver Whitecaps in the North American League at the invitation of assistant coach Alan Hinton. 'I was a bit wary at first, but it's a beautiful place and I had three great years out there. My two little girls were five and eight at the time, so it was new for them, but it was the right decision.'

The King enjoyed Astroturf-based soccer in the States and is proud of his 21 goals from 25 games in his first season – a record that still stands in Vancouver. He scored 15 in his second year as Vancouver lifted the Soccer Bowl, beating the star-spangled New York Cosmos along the way and Rodney Marsh's Fort Lauderdale in the Final. 'It was a thrill at that time to play against the likes of Beckenbauer and Cruyff,' he said. 'In fact I gave Beckenbauer a hard time. He was coming to the end of his career and I was still a bit sharp.'

From October to February for three seasons he returned home to play non-League football for Boston, Belper Town and then Burton Albion. 'I think I'd been playing at Burton for about a month, and then we got an FA Cup first-round game, and I told the manager Ian Storey-Moore to leave me out. I still wanted to play League football and didn't want to get Cup-tied, and, sure enough, a couple of days later I had a call from Colin Addison asking me to drop in to the Baseball Ground for a chat.

'I signed on for Derby again, but it was different by then. The only two players from the past were Roy and Stevie Powell. But it was still good to be back. I'd lost a bit of pace by that time and was playing mainly right side of midfield – we had Alan Biley and Dave Swindlehurst up front

'One of my best memories is my last game for Derby against Watford in 1982. We needed to win to stay up. I gave a daft penalty away – I dived in, which was totally unlike me – but I managed to get the equaliser and Kevin Wilson got the winner, so that was a nice way to go out. We won 3–2.'

Hector signs in 1966, watched by manager Tim Ward (left) and chairman Sam Longson.

The subject turned to today's footballers. 'Of course I would have loved to play today. I would have enjoyed the money to start with, but I would have loved to have played on pitches that look good all the way through the season. Also since the back-pass was thrown out it's given strikers more chances to score. I'd like to think with my pace I would have scored a few more goals.'

Kevin is used to Rams fans expressing surprise at his chosen career after football – that of postman. 'I looked after a pub for three years in the wilds of Ticknall, but I didn't enjoy it,' he says. 'I hate being stuck indoors. Then I saw an advert in the paper about the post. I applied and got the job, never thinking it would go on for more than 15 years, but I enjoyed it. It was sometimes a bit sticky in winter, but in the summer there is nothing like the post to keep the weight down.'

Ninety minutes on and Kevin had finally downed his pint. We shook hands, and as I watched him make his way home, sprightly as ever (he was still turning out for the ex-Rams in 2008), my mind went back to the school playground…a cross comes in from the left, I volley the ball towards the school gate (in my mind it is the Normanton goal) and as it flies into the net the Baseball Ground crowd roars, and for a brief moment once more I *am* Kevin Hector.

1973–74 **Ron Webster**

Bill Curry and Keith Havenhand were the goalscorers when 18-year-old Ron Webster made his Derby County debut in a 2–2 draw at Bury's Gigg Lane ground in the spring of 1962. A crowd of a little over 7,000 saw Ronnie – born and bred in Derbyshire (and proud of it!) – take his first tentative steps in an underrated career that would climax in two League Championships and an appearance record bettered by only one other Rams player.

Ron Webster.

Also in Harry Storer's side that March day in 1962 were Ilkeston-born Geoff Barrowcliffe, Derby-born Jack Parry and Ambergate-born Mick Hopkinson…that is the way it was back then. Season 1961–62 was also the last for one of Derby's most famous home-grown talents, Tommy Powell, as the Rams finished in the bottom half of the old Second Division and Storer retired to make way for a new manager, Tim Ward.

Ten years later, the Rams were champions of all England for the first time in their history, and at right-back the quietly spoken Webster missed only four games in a side transformed by Brian Clough's imported talent. The only other Derbyshire lad apart from Ron among the 16 players who made appearances in 1971–72 was Tommy Powell's son Steve.

Born in Belper but a resident of Somercotes and South Normanton all his life, Ron Webster never dreamed he would achieve not just one, but two League Championship medals in a career that started and finished at the Baseball Ground. He admits to me: 'It never crossed my mind to play for anyone else. Tottenham came in for me when I was younger, but I didn't want to go there because I've never liked big cities. I never even used to stay in Derby after home matches – I always used to come home.'

A marauding midfielder as a kid and the best player at his school, Ron achieved his childhood ambition of being signed by the Rams, but he wanted more. 'We were near the bottom of the table in the second half of that 1961–62 season and Harry Storer seemed to be giving everyone chances except me,' says Ron. 'So I went to see him one day and told him I thought I could do a better job, and the following Saturday he put me in at Bury.'

This is a rare example of tub-thumping by the reticent Webster, who adds: 'I never expected to get as far as being a professional footballer with Derby, but it was a great experience and I loved every minute of it.'

Though injury restricted Ron's progress in the next couple of seasons, new manager Ward kept faith in the hard-tackling wing-half, and between the start of the 1964 campaign and the arrival of Brian Clough in the summer of 1967 Webster hardly missed a game. 'The first day Cloughie came in he got us all sat down and told us if we stopped with him we would all be successful,' Ron recalls. 'He added if we didn't want to be successful we should go and see him. I remember sitting up and thinking

"Bloody hell!" The club wasn't doing anything, but he started talking about promotion from the first day, barking at us like a sergeant major.'

Only four players in the dressing room that day survived and thrived as Clough took an ailing club by the scruff of the neck: Webster, goalkeeper Colin Boulton, Welsh midfielder Alan Durban and striker Kevin Hector, an inspired Ward signing. A fifth, Peter Daniel, would play a major part only after Clough's departure.

Hector is the only player in Derby's history to have played more games than Webster – 589 against 535 – but there are no hard feelings from Ron. 'For 10 years I thought he was the best in whichever League we were in. He was real class. Everything was so easy for him, no effort and he was so quick – a really great player. He seemed to ride tackles and he was brilliant, but, to be honest, I played alongside a lot of brilliant players in those Championship seasons.'

As the Rams took the Second Division title in Clough's second season in charge, Webster had made the transition from midfielder to right-back. 'Jack Bowers told me I would be a better defender eventually, and after one season in midfield under Clough I went to full-back, and I enjoyed it there,' he says.

Ron is happy to confirm the story of being instructed by Clough to give Roy McFarland a roof over his head when he signed for the Rams in August 1967. 'Doreen and I had just got married in the June, but we were told by Cloughie to put Roy up for two or three months, and that was all right. I don't drink, and it's true Mick Hopkinson used to come and pick Roy up for trips to the pub, but we looked after him.'

A year before Derby fans celebrated promotion to the top flight in the summer of 1969 they were stunned by the capture of Dave Mackay from Tottenham Hotspur. 'I can't tell you what Dave's arrival did for everyone's confidence,' Ron tells me. 'I would have liked to have played with him when he was really good, but he was brilliant with all of us when he came to Derby. Everything he did was perfect.

A young Ron Webster pictured (back row, far left) in this team photo from the early 1960s.

He was a leader on the pitch and used to shout at us all the time. So with him shouting and Cloughie doing it as well, you couldn't go far wrong! We had Roy McFarland who won everything in the air and Mackay who wouldn't let anything through the middle, so all John Robson and I had to do was cover round and do our jobs, and we did that quite well,' says Ron, with typical understatement.

'After Mackay, Cloughie signed Willie Carlin, and that's when we started to play like a team. Willie was the final piece in the jigsaw. Cloughie got us all worked up and confident, so much so that we knew we were going to win before we went out onto the pitch. He used to breed confidence in everybody. He was a good man-manager. He didn't treat everyone the same; he knew how to work people up and he knew how to make players feel confident. Everyone is different, and Brian Clough treated everyone differently. He knew how to psyche you up and that's what he did, week after week.'

Ron is the first to admit he needed more convincing than most that he had the ability to succeed at the top level. 'I was enjoying myself because I never imagined we would reach the heights of the old First Division. I knew I

Webster goes through his paces at a muddy Baseball Ground.

could play in the Second Division, but when Cloughie came, anything was possible. I never thought I would get that far, but it was all down to him. I just felt lucky to be kept in there as long as I was.'

Webster was confirmed as a fixture in Clough's defence in the two seasons of top-flight consolidation that followed promotion, during which the Rams gave as good as they got against the likes of Bertie Mee's Arsenal, Bill Shankly's Liverpool and especially in the increasingly ill-tempered encounters with Don Revie's Leeds United.

A solitary defeat in their final eight games of the 1970–71 campaign gave a clue to what was to come as Derby fans said farewell to Mackay the player and welcomed his transfer record-breaking replacement Colin Todd. The unbeaten League run continued 12 games into the following campaign, and by the start of December 1971 the Rams were in contention for top honours alongside fellow title challengers Leeds, Liverpool and Manchester City.

So it was a massively important game as City, the flamboyant team of Bell, Summerbee and Lee, managed jointly by Bill Mercer and Malcolm Allison, arrived at the Baseball Ground on 4 December. The television cameras were there to capture a rare spectacle – a goal from Ron Webster, one of only seven scored throughout his distinguished Derby career. 'The best part of my game was defending,' he explains.

'I never went up for free-kicks or corners or anything like that. I enjoyed defending. That day against Manchester City I think I played it out to Ally Hinton and just kept running, and I thought "If it comes, so be it". When it did I just dived, and I think I shut my eyes as well! To tell you the truth it simply hit me on the head. My target in any match was all about goals conceded, not how many I scored, and I was happy to stop goals.'

The galloping celebration of a delighted Webster as the ball flew past City goalkeeper Joe Corrigan will live long in the memory of Rams fans who witnessed that goal, the first in a 3–1 victory. Bewilderment, surprise and delight were the chief emotions when news filtered through to the team camp in Majorca at the end of that memorable campaign that Liverpool and Leeds, both with a game in hand on Clough's side, had fluffed their chance and the title was Derby's. 'I remember waiting for the final results of the season to come in,' says Ron, 'and I have to say that Cloughie had put us in a frame of mind where we expected to be champions. We had done our job and couldn't do any more, and luckily it was our year.'

The following season featured European Cup adventures as the Rams reached the semi-finals against Juventus. A new teammate on the left side of the Derby defence arrived in the shape of the classy David Nish, signed from Leicester City for £225,000 to replace John Robson, while a young striker named Roger Davies, signed for a more modest £12,000 from non-League Worcester City, broke through, making his mark with a hat-trick at White Hart Lane in a remarkable 5–3 FA Cup replay come-back

Crowds line the streets of Matlock in April 1969 as Division Two champions Derby County make their triumphal tour of Derbyshire. Holding the trophy for the Rams are Ron Webster and Alan Durban.

against Tottenham. After the excitement of winning the title, however, seventh place in 1972–73 was somewhat of a disappointment for the expectant Derby faithful as Shankly's Liverpool took the top honour, despite taking only a point in their two League encounters against the Rams.

A decent start to the 1973–74 season, in which Derby were destined to finish third behind Liverpool and champions Leeds, served only to paper over the cracks of ever-widening divisions behind the scenes at the Baseball Ground as chairman Sam Longson sought to rein in the outspoken Clough. After beating Manchester United 1–0 at Old Trafford on 13 October, Clough and sidekick Peter Taylor sensationally resigned, prompting a player revolt and a protest movement among the fans.

Dave Mackay returned to restore a semblance of order, and one of the new manager's first decisions was to spend £80,000 on Swindon Town's Welsh international right-back Rod Thomas, but he rarely got a look-in as Webster retained his place in the team and was voted Player of the Year by the fans. 'I wasn't the best player in 1973–74,' says Ron. 'Colin Todd was phenomenal that year and it must have been something going through the crowd where they just decided to reward my loyalty. I had a good season, but Toddy should have won it by a mile. I wasn't as classy as the rest of the team, you see. I just did a job.'

Webster remained the first-choice number two as Mackay's Rams kicked-off their second Championship season, and the omens were good as early as 25 October as Derby mauled Chelsea 4–1 in a night-time match at the Baseball Ground. Among the goalscorers was Ron, who headed his first goal since the collector's item against Manchester City in the first title-winning campaign.

An injury sustained in an FA Cup third-round replay against Orient early in the New Year of 1975 finally let in Thomas, by which time Ron had become only the fifth player to complete 500 appearances for the Rams. Mainly cameo appearances remained for the reliable Webster, though he had a sustained run in the side under Mackay's managerial replacement Colin Murphy, playing at left-back towards the back-end of the 1976–77 season as cover for the injured Nish. In the 1–1 draw at Sunderland's Roker Park on 23 April 1977, Ron beat the legendary Steve Bloomer's 62-year-old club record of 525 appearances. He also enjoyed summers playing in the US for Minnesota Kicks before hanging up his boots to become Derby's youth coach in August 1978.

Ask him about his toughest opponents and Ron is typically unfazed. 'When we played against Manchester United George Best tended to play centre-forward, so I never actually came up against him directly. I marked a lad called John Aston and Best played down the middle against Roy and Toddy, so he rarely had a kick against us. We always subdued him one way or another. Tommy Hutchinson of Coventry was the hardest to get the ball off, but he used to try to beat you two or three times and I used to get him the second or third time! So he didn't achieve much.

'I couldn't really pick my most talented teammate. Colin Boulton was a great

Rams players (from left to right) Ron Webster, John McGovern, Alan Hinton, John Robson and Les Green with the Watney Cup, which they won on 8 August 1970 by beating Manchester United 4–1.

Derby County's players with manager Colin Addison (far left) and assistant manager John Newman (far right) at the Baseball Ground in August 1980. Former long-serving defender Ron Webster, then on the coaching staff, is next to Newman.

'keeper, Roy, Toddy, David Nish, John Robson, John O'Hare, Kevin, Ally, Archie…how can you possibly pick from that lot? If you really pushed me I would say Toddy, but they were all in their positions as good a player as you could wish to have.'

As for an analysis of his own contribution to the greatest teams in the club's history, Ron is predictably self-effacing. 'I just went out and gave my best – I couldn't do any more because I wasn't as skilful as the rest, most of whom were international players. I just took every match as it came. Comparing the two Championship-winning sides I would say Cloughie's side were harder to beat and were a better team, but Mackay's had better individual players.'

A 22-year relationship with Derby County ended abruptly for Ron in November 1982 when Peter Taylor returned as manager. Despite being a big Brian Clough fan, youth coach Webster had never hit it off with Taylor. 'Cloughie was brilliant, but I could never get on with Taylor, and when he was appointed manager I wouldn't have stopped at the club under any circumstances,' he says. 'I get on with most people, but he just wasn't my kind of person.'

Ron was perfectly happy to turn his back on football and work his Derbyshire farm, now run by his son, and he has little to do these days with the game that once played such a massive part in his life. 'Football is totally different now with the huge wages,' he says, 'but I wouldn't swap anything. I go to work in a chemicals factory my cousin owns in Alfreton. I enjoy it because I like to work.'

Do not assume that a man who played more than 500 times in the greatest Derby County teams in the club's history is constantly being pestered by workmates to talk about those glory years. 'There's hardly anyone knows who I am, and I don't mind that at all,' says Ron. 'Everything is in the past now. Even when I go to a match at Pride Park it's only the loyal fans that stand outside main reception who seem to know who I am. But I don't mind that.'

1974–75 **Peter Daniel**

You could be forgiven for not recognising the mild-mannered chap behind the counter at Hilltop Post Office in Eastwood. In fact, you could quite easily buy a book of stamps from Peter Daniel and walk away oblivious to the fact you had just done business with the fans' choice as best player in one of Derby County's most memorable seasons.

If you had taken the trouble to ask, he would have told you about marking George Best, scoring a fantastic goal at Stamford Bridge and, of course, being voted Player of the Year as the Rams claimed the League Championship under Dave Mackay in 1974–75. You will not find any clues to his success as a footballer at Peter's post office on the Notts-Derbys border, and that is typical of the modest, softly spoken life-long Rams fan who lived the dream.

Between 1964 and 1978 Peter played 237 games for Derby, often as a bit-part player during the halcyon days of Clough and Mackay. More often than not required to wait patiently in the shadows, he was utterly reliable when called upon.

Equally happy and dependable in either full-back position or at the heart of the defence, he stepped out of the shadows in his 10th season with the Rams to deputise throughout the campaign for one of the club's all-time greats, Roy McFarland. Derby fans, a knowledgeable bunch, voted him best player that season ahead of established stars such as Nish, Rioch, Todd, Gemmill, Lee and Hector.

Brought up in Stanley, a village midway between Derby and Ilkeston, he was always a Rams fan. 'From being small I always said I wanted to play for Derby County,' he tells me. 'I still remember one

Christmas getting everything I wanted: a pair of football boots and a Derby County shirt and shorts.'

Signed as an apprentice by Tim Ward, Peter bagged a lift to the Baseball Ground in the early days with Geoff Barrowcliffe, a fixture at full-back for the previous 12 seasons. 'I had to be in half an hour before the pros and do all the usual chores, including cleaning all the boots,' he says.

Peter made his debut at left-back on 2 October 1965 in 2–1 home win against Bristol City. In his match report in the *Derby Evening Telegraph*, Gerald Mortimer wrote of Peter: '…he had a most satisfactory debut. A big occasion was thrust on him suddenly when Ray Young reported unfit, but he showed surprising assurance for an 18-year-old with only a limited amount of Central League appearances.'

Peter did not miss another game that season, playing 35 times including an FA Cup third round

Peter Daniel.

Peter Daniel with arms full of silverware, celebrating the 1971–72 Championship success with (from left to right) Archie Gemmill, Terry Hennessey, John O'Hare and Ron Webster.

2–5 home reversal against Manchester United in January 1966 when he was called upon to mark a prodigiously talented young winger by the name of George Best. Although Best scored twice that day, the Irishman was eventually reined in. It was not to be the last Best versus Daniel tussle.

Brian Clough swept into town like a whirlwind in the summer of 1967, and Peter played 22 times in Cloughie's first season – every game at full-back – as the Rams finished a modest 18th in the old Second Division.

Then McFarland, Mackay, Ron Webster and John Robson established themselves as the first choice back-four in the promotion season that followed, and Peter had to wait until the 13th game of the top-flight campaign to get his chance, against Manchester United in front of almost 41,000 fans at the Baseball Ground.

'On that particular day I was down to play for the reserves, but the manager phoned me to say Ron Webster had failed a fitness test and to get down to the Baseball Ground as fast as I could, because he needed me to mark George Best,' recalls Peter. 'I did as I was told and got caught speeding on my way to the ground! There were two policemen; one was a Derby fan and the other, the one who booked me, clearly wasn't! Anyway, I think I did OK because we beat Manchester United 2–0. Best was a phenomenal player who could go past you like you weren't there, but I got a few tackles in, and thankfully he decided to play more down the middle that day.'

Still Peter had to wait patiently in the wings, not being called on at all during the first League Championship campaign of 1971–72 when the Rams' Player of the Year was a new defender, Colin Todd, signed by Clough for a record £170,000. In Todd and McFarland, Derby now had the best central-defenders around. As Mackay returned as boss following Clough's shock resignation in October 1973, there was no clue that Peter would be part of the new manager's plans.

Then in May 1974 everything changed when McFarland snapped an Achilles tendon while playing for England at Wembley. 'Roy was a friend, and still is, and I wouldn't have wished that injury on him,' says Peter, 'but I was ready to step in. I was relieved when Dave Mackay told us he wouldn't be buying anyone in to replace Roy. I was on the team sheet for the first game of the season against Everton, and it felt good.'

Alongside him was Todd – the quickest and most powerful defender in England. 'Going into that season Toddy's instructions to me were very simple. He told me to attack every ball and not to worry because he would pick up the pieces. And he did.'

Two moments stand out for Peter from that Championship campaign. 'Early in the New Year we played Liverpool at the Baseball Ground and were really under the cosh against their strikers Keegan and Toshack,' he says. 'They were streaming forward, but I remember getting in a good tackle just inside our half and moving forward with the ball. Kevin Hector was in space wide on the right and everyone expected me to pass to him but I managed to thread a ball down the middle to Franny Lee who smashed it in. We won 2–0.'

'The other memory is when we beat Chelsea 2–1 at Stamford Bridge in the March. We won possession and, probably because I'd scored the previous week against Tottenham, I decided to head up field.'

Gerald Mortimer again takes up the story from his *Evening Telegraph* report of the game: 'Daniel and Gemmill won the ball on the edge of their own penalty area and Gemmill hurtled off on a long run before finding Davies on the left...Enter Daniel, who had never stopped running and had never been picked up by a Chelsea defender. The ball came to him a little awkwardly but he was able to

Steve Powell in high-flying action in the 2–2 draw against Norwich City at the Baseball Ground in October 1977. Kevin Hector and Peter Daniel are to the right of the picture. Gerry Daly is the other Rams player.

propel it in the right direction for his second goal in successive matches. Before this season, Daniel had played 136 matches without scoring. Now he has four goals to his name, none of them more important than this.'

Equally eventful was the night Peter collected the Jack Stamps Trophy at the club's awards evening at Bailey's Nightclub in Derby. The Rams had just one more game to play, and only Ipswich Town could overhaul them at the top by winning a game in hand that same night at Manchester City's Maine Road. 'We were sitting down to eat when news came through that we were champions,' Peter recalls. 'People were dancing up and down and we never did get to eat the food!'

There was talk of harsh treatment towards the Player of the Year when the fit-again

Daniel on the ball at the Baseball Ground.

McFarland returned for the last three games of that memorable campaign, but Peter is happy to set the record straight. 'In pre-season I had torn a pelvic muscle, and I survived the whole season on pain killers,' he explains. 'I hardly did any training – I just played the games. Over Easter we had four games in nine days, and I was at the end of my tether. Fortunately, Roy got back to fitness at that time. It was five or six weeks into the next season before my injury finally healed and I was able to play again.'

Peter left his beloved Derby for Vancouver Whitecaps in 1978, returning after two seasons to play with Burton Albion and then Belper Town. After quitting the game he ran a paper shop before moving into the post office at Eastwood. 'I don't get to see many Derby games because I work until 1 o'clock on Saturdays,' he says. 'In the early days not many of the customers knew my background, and that was probably just as well, because this is Forest territory. When they did find out they had a bit of a go at me, but in a good-natured way.'

No one could give such a thoroughly pleasant man as Peter Daniel a hard time. Not even George Best!

1975–76 **Charlie George**

The fact that Charlie George had his left arm in a sling when he received the Player of the Year award at the end of the 1975–76 season told its own story. The freak injury, sustained in a bad-tempered game against Stoke City at the Baseball Ground on a March evening in 1976, not only meant a premature end to an often pulsating campaign for the best player in the country at that time, it is still recognised by many Derby County aficionados as the single piece of misfortune that precipitated the steep decline of the club over the next 10 years.

'Their centre-half Denis Smith was playing the ball, and I went to block it, and as he whacked it he sort of got out of the way,' Charlie tells me. 'So I didn't hit him, and as I landed my shoulder popped out, and I'll tell you what, it was one of the worst injuries I can remember. Franny Lee was in the dressing room and he said "I thought you Londoners were hard!" But every little movement killed. The doctor tried to put it back into place in the dressing room but he couldn't, so I had to go to hospital,

Charlie George (centre) signs for the Rams, pictured with Derby County secretary Stuart Webb (left), and manager Dave Mackay (right). London, 2 July 1975.

and it wasn't until three days later that I found out I'd fractured my elbow as well. It was very disappointing for me the way that season finished, but these things happen.'

That Stoke City encounter came just 10 days before an FA Cup semi-final against Manchester United at Hillsborough, and at the time the Rams were also in the hunt for a second consecutive Championship under Dave Mackay.

Without George, who had hit the back of the net 24 times at an average of better than a goal every other game since being snapped up for a bargain £100,000 at the start of the campaign from his beloved Arsenal, Derby massively under-performed in losing 2–0 to United in the Cup semi-final, and managed to win just two of their six remaining League matches to finish fourth behind United, Queen's Park Rangers and champions Liverpool.

With the addition of George and record signing Leighton James, Mackay's side of 1975–76 had even more flair than his Championship-winning team of the previous season, and it is still a source of regret to Charlie that no silverware was won to support such a thrilling campaign that included a hat-trick for the striker in a European Cup defeat of mighty Real Madrid.

When early in 2008 Robbie Savage, once the player the Derby crowd most loved to hate from his days with East Midlands neighbours Leicester City, joined the Rams, many yelled that the signing was ill-advised. Rewind 33 years and Charlie George arrived at the Baseball Ground to similar grumbles. The long-haired lad from London (his famous barnet was permed by the time he made the move to Derby) had acquired a bad boy reputation, having fallen out with Arsenal boss Bertie Mee. As a Gunners player he had also taken every opportunity to wind up the Baseball Ground crowd and had not been averse to giving them a special salute on occasions!

Charlie celebrates with Bruce Rioch at the Baseball Ground.

'I was on the Highbury terraces from five years of age, and Arsenal were my local team and always will be, and that will never change,' says Charlie, 'but I have very fond memories of Derby. I had some great times there, played with some fantastic players and the support was great, especially considering I'd scored a couple of goals against Derby, had verbals with the crowd and used to have kick-ups with the Derby players! So when I went there I think first of all it was a bit different, but once they found out I could play the game there was no problem.

'In the old days the supporters were used to having a bit of banter with the players, more than they do now, but of course the players were closer to the supporters then than they ever are now. The most important thing is the people watching wanted to see if you could play the game, and they would soon find you out if you couldn't. Luckily enough I wasn't too bad at it!'

When it became common knowledge in the summer of 1975 that Charlie was surplus to

Charlie George with physio Gordon Guthrie and assistant manager Des Anderson after dislocating his shoulder in 1976.

requirements at Arsenal (the Gunners had finished seventh bottom as the Rams lifted their second Championship in three years), Mackay interrupted a holiday in Scotland to sign him for Derby. 'When Dave came down we did the deal in about 20 minutes,' Charlie recalls. 'It wasn't Arsenal I'd fallen out with, unfortunately it was the manager I didn't get on with. I met Dave and all I wanted was to play football for someone who wanted me. Tottenham had come in for me the day before. Terry Neil was their manager and I had a bit of a medical there. They said they were coming back to me, but it dragged on a bit and when Dave came in I just wanted to get it all sorted. It would have been easier for me to move to Tottenham, not that it would have gone down very well with the Arsenal supporters, but sometimes you don't do the obvious things in life. I have no regrets whatsoever about joining Derby rather than Tottenham.'

Football's *enfant terrible* made his Derby debut at Wembley in the Charity Shield victory over West Ham in August 1975. 'I didn't play too badly that day and we won, which is always nice in your first competitive game for a new club,' says Charlie.

Playing in a fluid front three with Kevin Hector and Franny Lee (Leighton James would add width to the side on his arrival from Burnley in the autumn), George was in his element. 'Kevin Hector was one of the great goalscorers. You don't realise how good people are until you actually play with them, and he was a phenomenal goalscorer, there's no doubt about that. He was a very, very fit lad as well. Then of course there was Franny, the roly-poly guy who understood the game and was a tremendous player as well, and of course me, probably not the most conformist player in the world, and we really hit it off. We just played football.

'But look at that side! You start from the back with Tommo (Rod Thomas), Roy, Toddy and Nishy, and then you had Archie and Henry (Newton) and Bruce in midfield, plus Stevie Powell…whoever came in just wanted to play football and it was great. Nothing was too complicated – we just said "let's get the ball and play". The only regret I have is that we didn't win anything in that first season, because I honestly believe if I hadn't got injured against Stoke we would have gone on and won the double, for the simple reason we took three points off Man United that season, but I couldn't play in the FA semi against them, and eventually we finished fourth in the League. We weren't frightened of anybody, and it was a big disappointment not to win anything. But these things happen in life, and you have to move on.'

A goal on his League debut against Sheffield United at Bramall Lane a week after the Charity Shield victory was a nice way to start, and I was on the front row of the Normanton End terracing to see Charlie benefit from one of the most comic moments I ever witnessed at the Baseball Ground, when Manchester United visited in the September. With five minutes remaining and the scores level at one apiece, United goalkeeper Alex Stepney, having collected a routine through ball, contemplated rolling the ball out to his left-back but changed his mind mid-roll. Unfortunately for him, his brain failed to fully engage with his arm and he succeeded only in spilling the ball to the feet of Charlie who, alert as ever, accepted the gift to clinch victory with his second goal of the game.

Four weeks later I was back in the Normanton End terracing to witness *the* Charlie George goal as Real Madrid arrived in Derby for the first-leg tie in the second round of the European Cup. A crisp left-foot volley from the edge of the area gave the illustrious visitors' goalkeeper Miguel no chance and

Charlie has just scored in the 1–1 draw against West Brom at the Baseball Ground in October 1977.

inspired BBC match commentator Barry Davies to scream: 'Oooh that's a cracker! That's the best first time shot you'll ever see!'

Charlie, predictably, plays it down. 'For a start Archie probably mis-hit the cross from the left, and yes it was a good goal, but I think sometimes people make mountains out of molehills. I just put my foot to the ball – and I was very lucky because I could strike a ball – and it's timing more than anything. It was a sort of pass into the back of the net. Night matches in Derby had a special atmosphere and you can imagine the Real Madrid players getting off the bus at the Baseball Ground with all the terraced housing down there and thinking "Bloody hell – what's this?" They had a fantastic team of internationals: Del Bosque was the captain and ended up managing the club, as did Comacho, who also played. Then there was Santillano, the Spanish centre-forward, together with other top players like Pirri and the German internationals Breitner and Netzer, who played in the middle of the park.'

George completed a hat-trick that memorable October night (the other two goals both came from penalties) and one more from David Nish gave the Rams a seemingly unassailable 4–1 lead going into the second leg in front of a crowd of 120,000 at the Bernabeu on Bonfire Night. Unfortunately, all the fireworks came from Real Madrid as the Rams, despite another George goal, went down 5–1 after extra-time. 'I think I must be the only player to score four goals against Real Madrid and be on the bloody losing side!' Charlie laughs. 'The one in Madrid was probably the best of the four, but no one talks about that one because we got beat.

'That Saturday we went to Arsenal and won 1–0; Kevin Hector scored the goal. For me it was just like playing against my mates in a training session because we used to kick the hell out of each other in training at Arsenal anyway! A lad came on the pitch with a big bouquet of flowers for me and I think I got a fantastic cheer. I was very lucky, you know, because I had a great rapport with the supporters there, especially the North Bank, because I probably knew half of them!'

Charlie George and Irish international goalkeeper Ron Healey confront each other at the Baseball Ground in May 1982, in a game which ended 0–0.

Charlie is a special guest as Derby play Arsenal in the last game at the Baseball Ground, May 1997.

What playing colleagues at Derby say about Charlie George is that he was supremely talented and nothing like the troublemaker depicted in some areas of the media. 'I am a Cockney and proud of it, but everyone liked to portray me as something I wasn't. I was no angel, let's not get away from that little fact, but deep down I think I was quite a nice person and I generally got on with everybody. I never had a problem with anyone,' says Charlie.

Apart, that is, from England managers.

The clamour for international recognition for a player who had been marked out as a future England star since breaking through to the Arsenal first team as a teenager grew louder after his brilliant first season with the Rams. Don Revie bowed to public pressure and picked George against the Republic of Ireland the following season. 'I started out in the middle of the park and, watching the match later on TV I thought I was one of the better players,' Charlie remembers. 'But he said to me at half-time he wanted me to start going down the left-wing. I told him I wasn't a left-winger, but that's what he wanted. The funny thing is that 15 minutes into the second-half Gordon Hill, who was a left-winger, started warming up so I knew I was coming off. And when Revie substituted me he went to shake my hand, but unfortunately me being Charlie I just told him what I thought and walked straight up the tunnel. I know I should have played more than 60 minutes for England. I mean, was Stuart Pearson a better player than me? I don't think so. But it happens. Revie eventually went to Saudi Arabia for more money and Ron Greenwood took over and wanted me to play for the B team. I told him I wasn't playing for the B team and that was the end of Charlie. But you know, you make a decision and you have to stand by it.'

Hat-tricks in 1976–77 against Tottenham in the League and against Finn Harps in a record-breaking 12–0 UEFA Cup first-round home leg victory at the Baseball Ground contributed towards 17 goals in all that campaign, but the fizz had gone out of Derby County and something seemed to have disappeared from Charlie's game. Mackay's departure in November 1976 did little for team morale, and by Christmas George had a new strike partner in Derek Hales, a speculative record-breaking capture from Second Division Charlton Athletic. Though prolific in the lower Leagues, Hales soon lost confidence in the top flight, and after two scintillating seasons Derby were a mile short in 1976–77, finishing 20 points behind champions Liverpool and only three clear of relegated Sunderland, Stoke and Tottenham.

The Derby board fluttered its eyelashes at Brian Clough, but the former boss stayed put at Nottingham Forest while Colin Murphy battled it out in the hot seat at the Baseball Ground, before being replaced by Tommy Docherty early in 1977–78 as the Rams failed to register a victory in their

Charlie, from the penalty spot, on his way to a hat-trick against Real Madrid.

opening seven League games. 'I never had a problem with Tommy Docherty,' says Charlie, 'but I think at the time he sold too many of our players. Once we got our bearings with each other we were okay, and he never said too much to me.'

Charlie still managed to get into double figures in the scoring charts as Derby recovered to a mid-table finish in 1977–78, the season former boss Clough took his promoted Forest to the title with a seven-point advantage over second-placed Liverpool. By the December of the following season Charlie had gone, sold by Docherty to Southampton for £400,000. The striker returned briefly as a free agent towards the end of the 1981–82 season, brought in by manager John Newman, and scored twice in 11 games to help stave off the real threat of relegation from the Second Division.

These days Charlie works at Arsenal as a star host at the Emirates Stadium. Ask him to nominate his favourite teammate from the glory years and, like every other Derby player from the 1970s, he struggles. 'Toddy was my old roommate, and he was a fantastic player. Rod Thomas is an old mate too who used to live in the same hotel as me for a time – he was a tremendous long-legged player who was very difficult to get around. David Nish too was a cultured football and Roy McFarland – what can you say? When our back four got the ball they could keep it for half an hour to keep the pressure off you, because they were all quality players.

'In midfield you had Archie Gemmill, and I've never seen a guy as fit as him in my life, plus he was a winner with a little bit of grit about him. Then there was Bruce (Rioch). I mean, I thought I could strike a ball, but I think Bruce might have struck it harder than me, and then Henry (Newton) or Stevie Powell in the middle of the park, workers for the team. Leighton (James) came in too and we had a good footballing team, and when you look at those players you think "Bloody hell, there was a lot of quality there".

'I will always hold Derby in high regard. I know people in London who support Derby, and the club will always be special to me because I enjoyed my football there so much and respected every player I played with. I had a fantastic time up there.'

Finally, he muses again about that fateful injury sustained at the Baseball Ground against Stoke City on the night of 24 March 1976. 'It was fantastic to be Player of the Year in 1975–76, but the only thing was that when I went to collect the trophy I had my arm in a sling,' he says. 'Ideally I'd have liked to have had my arm out of a sling because then I could have held the trophy in one hand and had a drink at the same time!'

1976–77 **Leighton James**

Illustrating the intimacy of the old Baseball Ground, particularly for those who played on the wing, Leighton James laughs as he tells a joke against himself. 'I can remember one game running down the left wing and cutting inside to have a shot that went closer to the corner flag than it did the goal and some wag in the crowd shouted "Bloody hell Jesse James, that's no bloody good!" And his mate turned to him and screamed "Hey, bloody Jesse James could shoot straight. He can't!"

'I was lucky in my career that I played for two clubs – Derby County and Swansea City – that probably had the most intimidating grounds, the Baseball Ground and the Vetch Field. You would never want to be a visiting player at those places. To me they were like the old chicken run, the old scratching shed. They were grounds that as a home player you knew the opposition weren't looking forward to coming to. As a player you looked forward to playing at the big arenas like White Hart Lane, Highbury and Old Trafford to portray your skills on the big stage. But in the middle of winter when it felt like the Baseball Ground was knee-deep in mud it was tremendous in terms of atmosphere and the crowd being literally on top of you, especially when Derby were playing well.'

Leighton James with Dave Mackay.

When Dave Mackay paid Burnley £310,000 for James in November 1975 to further strengthen the reigning champions of English football, yet another club transfer record was broken.

The Welsh international was an out-and-out winger in the mould of Alan Hinton, a player still on Derby's books but restricted to a bit-part role in 1974–75 as Mackay's side romped to the League title with an instinctive forward line of Franny Lee, Roger Davies and Kevin Hector. Though Hector and Lee were not averse to seeking out the greener pastures down the flanks at the Baseball Ground, neither was a winger in the old-fashioned sense.

When James arrived the following season to add pizazz to an entertaining side already energised by the capture of the irresistible Charlie George from Arsenal in the summer of 1975, Mackay had an abundance of creative riches at his disposal. 'It was a great honour to be

The Welsh wizard in Derby's side.

signed by such a great player and manager as Dave Mackay,' Leighton tells me. 'It was very good for the ego and very good for the confidence. I suppose £300,000 in those days probably equates to £30 million today because of the vastly inflated prices of the modern era, but I went very happily to Derby County.

'I would be a liar if I said it didn't put pressure on me because I was the highest priced player around, and £300,000 was a lot of money. You don't consciously feel the pressure but you do feel you have to come up with the goods, and I admit I took a little while to settle in. I wasn't an instant success, and to be deemed worthy of that kind of transfer fee you had to take the place by storm overnight and I didn't. But once I settled in I felt very comfortable and I certainly believed I began to justify the fee.'

It was a joke at the time that Derby were so good their record signing couldn't get into the side. Roger Davies was also struggling to get a look-in as Mackay went for a front three of Lee, Hector and George as the Rams stayed in contention with the other main front-runners, Liverpool, Queen's Park Rangers and Manchester United, throughout the first half of the 1975–76 campaign. James finally made his debut as a substitute for Henry Newton in a 2–1 defeat at Birmingham on 6 December. From then on he barely missed a game for the next two years until Tommy Docherty controversially swapped him for QPR's Don Masson.

It still excites Leighton to talk about that 1975–76 side – arguably even better than the Championship winners of the previous season and a good bet for the League and FA Cup double going into the last month of the campaign. 'Oh yes, I had just the odd one or 10 incredible teammates,' he says. 'Dave's side wasn't necessarily better than Brian Clough's side, but in terms of actual flair and match winners in the team we probably had more than the first Championship side. They were better organised, whereas we were off-the-cuff players, Charlie, myself, Franny Lee, Archie (Gemmill), Bruce Rioch – unbridled talent! The Derby County side of the early '70s was superb, better organised defensively and I'm sure trained towards keeping clean sheets, which we didn't do much work on. They were more tuned into winning games 1–0. We had a side in 1975–76 that said to the opposition if you score two we'll score three. That was the difference in the approach. Brian Clough was probably one of the greatest managers of all time, and he knew if his sides scored once they could still win, whereas if Dave's side scored only one, we might get a draw or lose.'

Leighton remains, however, a huge admirer of Hinton, the leading goalscorer in the 1971–72 side. 'Alan Hinton didn't beat people on the run but was by far and away the best crosser I have ever seen in my life and I count all the quality wingers who played at that time – Gordon Hill, Steve Coppell and me – Alan was better than all of us. He had a great skill of shifting the ball to one side and getting it around the defender. He was very much like David Beckham in that respect. Wingers like me and John Robertson would drop our shoulders and go past defenders, but Alan would just move the ball to one side and had an incredible ability to get it into the danger area. Beckham is a wonderful crosser of the ball and Alan was equally as good, and probably better in that he could do it with either foot whereas Beckham only uses his right.'

But when it comes to giving the vote for his most talented teammate at Derby, Leighton is unequivocal. 'Charlie George in terms of out and out ability was the best I ever played with,' he says. 'He had everything. He was quick, good in the air in terms of flicking things on, he had great presence, great skill with both feet and he could certainly strike a ball.

'I was actually at the game when Don Revie gave him his only cap and stuck him on the left wing. We had become good friends by then and we had an understanding on the field; I would know what he was going to do. When you train around class you get used to thinking like them, and I was training with some class players throughout my time at Derby. When I look at some of the people in that era who played many times for England, I would have felt insulted to have been given only got two-thirds of a match like Charlie was. At that time he was better than any other centre-forward in England. He would do things that ordinary players couldn't do. He was a phenomenally underrated player and a good pro who trained hard and was nothing like the public portrayal of the long-haired wide boy from London who no one could handle. Nothing could have been further from the truth.'

With George oozing class and James well into his speedy stride, the 1975–76 season was approaching its climax when it all went wrong on a Wednesday night late in March against Stoke City at the Baseball Ground. George dislocated a shoulder, and his season was over. The Rams, still flying high in the League, went into the FA Cup semi-final against Manchester United at Hillsborough 10 days later without their talisman, and Leighton is the first to admit that several other players also went missing that day. 'We were probably the biggest under-achievers in the world in that match, yet despite playing very poorly as a team we were denied a clear-cut equaliser by the referee Jack Taylor when David Nish beat the offside trap. Myself and a lot of other players failed to perform that day, but had we scraped a replay out of that game, which we didn't deserve, I have no doubt we would have beaten United. They had their one chance and they took it.'

Two goals from United's left-winger, Gordon Hill – later a Rams player – precipitated the start of a dramatic decline for the club. In the League, Derby conceded 12 goals in their remaining five games and won only once, a 6–2 final-game riot of goals at Ipswich's Portman Road as Franny Lee signed off at the end of a thrilling career with a brace. From title contenders they slipped to fourth place as Liverpool pipped QPR for top spot by a point.

'The after-effect of that semi-final defeat was probably the debacle of the following season when we started badly, including a 5–1 defeat at Birmingham when Kenny Burns scored four for them and I scored our goal,' says Leighton. 'Really the writing was on the wall for the manager after that result.'

Ironically the next match, the Rams' first win in the opening nine fixtures, was an extravagant 8–2 home thrashing of Tottenham – relegated as the bottom club in the First Division that season – but it was not enough to save Mackay and his assistant Des Anderson, who were dismissed in November, just 18 months after guiding Derby to the Championship. Board members at the Baseball Ground still harboured ambitions of bringing back Clough from neighbouring Nottingham Forest, and in the meantime reserve-team coach Colin Murphy was asked to take charge of first-team affairs. At the time Forest were a Second Division side, but in February 1977 – just 14 months before they won the League Championship in their first season back in the top flight – Clough and Peter Taylor announced they were staying at the City Ground, and Murphy was given the Derby job full-time.

'To be fair to Colin, he not only steadied the ship, he rescued it,' says Leighton. 'He was totally different to Dave. He was very organised and less off the cuff, and at that time it's probably what we needed. We didn't need another big name manager coming in to appease the ego of a few people, we needed someone like Colin, and we stayed up quite comfortably after struggling early on.'

As Liverpool picked up a second consecutive League title, the Rams finished 15th. It would be 12 years before they would get anywhere near to being a top-five side again among the elite of English football. But for Leighton James, who scored 15 goals in an exhausting 55 League and Cup matches that campaign, including a hat-trick in the record-breaking 12–0 UEFA Cup first-round hammering of Irish side Finn Harps, 1976–77 holds fond memories. 'Derby is a great club, and I thoroughly enjoyed my time there, and it is a great honour to have been voted Player of the Year that season,' he says. 'My name appears on that trophy alongside some absolutely world-class names, so I am very proud indeed to be on that list of honour. You could pick a very good side from that lot!'

Only six games into the 1977–78 season and manager Murphy was on his way out to be replaced by Tommy Docherty, the former Manchester United manager who had orchestrated Derby's semi-final defeat at Hillsborough 17 months earlier. By May 1979, when 'The Doc' resigned to take charge of QPR, the club's second Championship-winning squad had been all but decimated in a havoc of transfer dealings that saw the departure of crowd pleasers such as Hector, Todd, George, Gemmill and James, the subject of probably the most bizarre of Docherty's transfer dabbles, in October 1977. The Welshman, only 24 and arguably still shy of his prime, was swapped for 31-year-old Scottish midfielder Don Masson, who would play only 26 games in a Derby County shirt before being moved on to one of his former clubs Notts County. Though still good enough to make the Scotland squad for the 1978 World Cup finals in Argentina, Masson was approaching the end of his career, while James, who would eventually win 54 caps for Wales, was still playing first-class football 11 years later.

'Personally, I felt it was inexplicable that Derby should bring Docherty in,' says Leighton. 'It was bizarre and I still don't understand that appointment to this day. He was the architect of breaking up the team. He was hell-bent on bringing his own young players into the club. He didn't want senior pros around who, in his opinion, were likely to upset the apple cart because he'd had problems with a few of the older players at Manchester United. The fact he couldn't handle them was neither here nor there. He was opinionated to say the least, and he didn't want me and other players around who he couldn't dominate. We all know what happened next: Derby County went down the divisions.'

James's spell in London was brief. After 28 games for QPR he returned to Burnley in 1978 before joining Swansea City's extraordinary surge from the old Third Division to the First Division under John Toshack's management. He had spells with Sunderland, Bury and Newport County before joining Burnley for a third spell in 1986 as youth-team manager and occasional first-team player, eventually retiring three years later. His coaching career took Leighton to Bradford City before his appointment as manager of non-League Gainsborough Trinity in 1993. He later managed Morecambe and also had two spells in charge of League of Wales club Llanelli, and in 2001–02 he coached Garden Village of the Welsh Football League to the Second Division Championship title.

Never short of an opinion, the colourful James is a football pundit for BBC radio and television and is also a regular voice on *Real Radio*. When he controversially wrote in his *South Wales Evening Post* sports column that he hoped Barnsley would beat Cardiff City in the 2008 FA Cup semi-final, the public outcry prompted the BBC to suspend him for a period. Swansea-mad James's comments even inspired the song *Leighton James Don't Like Us*, recorded by Cardiff musician Leigh Bailey.

Not that Leighton will ever be short of a job. In the summer of 2007 he was voted Rookie Lollipop Man of the Year by Swansea City Council for his work at the school he attended as a child, Penyrheol Primary. 'A mate of mine works for the council's road safety department, and we were chatting one day about the shortage of lollipop men and women,' says Leighton. 'I asked him what it entailed, and when he told me I offered my services at my old junior school for a couple of weeks until they found someone more permanent. That was three years ago, and I still do the job every morning and every afternoon, dressed in a bright yellow t-shirt or a coat if it's raining. I think the motorists have a game: "Who can knock Leighton down first?"!'

So does the man who evaded the crunching lunge of many a hard-tackling right-back fear for his safety? 'I'm not as quick as I used to be,' he admits, 'but I'm cleverer. I see things coming a bit quicker than I used to!'

Leighton James.

1977–78 **David Langan**

I have a David Langan memory that has stayed with me since 1977, the year he broke through to the first team, with a debut against Leeds United three days before his 20th birthday.

In those days the pre-match warm-up was a leisurely affair a couple of minutes before kick-off. The Derby strikers would find their range by hitting balls towards Colin Boutlon's goal from the edge of the box at the Normanton End of the Baseball Ground, while the rest of the team jogged and stretched.

Rather than being prompted by an over-zealous PA announcer, the Popsiders and Ossie Enders would chant the song of each Rams player in turn…'Zigger Zagger, Zigger Zagger, Kevin Hector!' and, especially in 1977, 'Charlie, Charlie, Charlie Charleee, Charlie's the King of Derby!' Each player would acknowledge the chant with a wave to the crowd, and the ritual warmed up both the players and the watching faithful.

Way down the pecking order was the chant for young David Langan. Never have I seen a professional footballer look so acutely embarrassed to hear his name called out. Nor have I ever witnessed a more self-conscious acknowledgement. A flick of the hand; blink and you missed it.

The shy lad from Dublin just could not wait for the game to start – but once it did the crowd could be sure of a whole-hearted display from a slightly built full-back whose bravery and determination as a player have left their mark on him today.

Registered disabled with chronic knee and back problems, Dave works as a porter at the Town Council offices in Peterborough, his last port of call as a player. 'I was only 15 when I came across for the first trial with Brian Clough,' he tells me. 'It went well for me, and he signed me on as an apprentice, but I was lucky there were two or three Irish lads there at the time because I was very homesick and I missed my mum and dad a lot.

'Cloughie was very good to me. He used to give all the young lads £10 to take home at Christmas to buy mum a bunch of flowers. He'd tell us he would know if the flowers didn't arrive. I actually gave my mum the £10 because we were short of money and told her if anyone asked she must say I had bought her flowers!'

Langan was still an untried apprentice when Clough and Taylor resigned in the autumn of 1973 to be replaced by Dave Mackay. Although he had never seen the great Mackay as a player out on the pitch, the youngster was immediately impressed by the new manager's footballing ability. 'I remember Dave messing about with a ball in the indoor playing area at Raynesway,' he says. 'I used to watch him with amazement as he smacked a ball against a wall and then turned around and back-headed it against the wall and just kept it going. What he did with a ball was

David Langan in action for the Rams.

impossible; it was incredible to see. He must have been one of the greatest footballers ever because I've never seen anything like it. We used to play five-a-side, and he had an incredible will to win. If his side was losing, even at his age, he used to put himself about.'

Dave stayed in the background as, guided by Mackay, Derby won their second Championship in three years. When Mackay failed to win a vote of confidence from the board of directors after a poor start to the 1976–77 campaign (his managerial record in the League over the previous three seasons had been third, first and fourth) it opened the door for Langan, who had impressed reserve-team coach Colin Murphy, the man charged with following Mackay into the Derby hot seat. 'Dave left under a cloud, and then Colin took over and gave me my debut against Leeds. Colin was a very good coach and organiser, whereas with Dave you just went out and played. Colin didn't have a lot of respect from certain players and that was probably his downfall in the end, but he was very good to me, and I liked the man.

'My debut game was nearly called off. The night before the Baseball Ground was a mud heap because it chucked it down. There was a morning inspection, and I thought I wouldn't be playing so I wouldn't have to worry, but then the news came through that the game was on and Colin told me I would be marking Eddie Gray. I thought "Oh my God!". But when the team sheets came in Eddie was injured and not playing so I had no one to mark and Toddy and Roy Mac looked after me. The atmosphere was incredible, and on my first touch of the ball my stomach churned, but as the game went on the better I became, and I loved the atmosphere the fans created.'

Although Leeds won that day with the only goal of the game, Langan was in the side again the following week and about to consolidate his place at right-back. Ron Webster was coming to the end of a long and distinguished career, and such was Langan's impact – he barely missed a game throughout the next three-and-a-half seasons – Rod Thomas was allowed to depart to Cardiff City.

Langan's second game was at Anfield against the reigning champions – and Liverpool were well on their way to recording back-to-back League titles that year. 'We went a goal up from Kevin Hector as I remember, but they beat us 3–1,' says Dave. 'Still things went quite well for me that day because I marked Steve Heighway, and I kept my place in the team.'

Of all the left-wingers around at that time, Dave recalls that West Bromwich Albion's Willie Johnstone gave him the most trouble. 'He had so much speed and was a real handful, especially in one of the Cup matches, but Leighton James was a big help because as a left-winger himself he used to fill me in before matches on what my opponent would do. In any case, I had Toddy behind me with his pace so they couldn't really get round the back of us.'

Season 1977–78 is remembered by many Rams supporters as the time when Tommy Docherty arrived and set about ripping apart the second Championship-winning side. For Langan, 1977–78 has happier memories. In a campaign where 32 different players turned out for the first team, he was an ever present in a side that achieved mid-table respectability. Moreover, he was the fans' choice as Player of the Year.

'The awards night was at Bailey's Nightclub, and when they told me I had won the Jack Stamps Trophy I thought they were joking,' Dave recalls. 'But they weren't and said I'd better get a speech prepared! Tommy Docherty called me up to the stage, and I just didn't know what to say. I just couldn't believe it; I was star-struck. All those incredible players in the room and I was the Player of the Year! I would hate to think what the players I played with in those days would be worth on the transfer market if they were playing today. Priceless. That was probably the greatest team I ever played with, and they were nice lads too, no prima donnas, and they helped me out. Charlie George was so down to earth. I'd heard he was flash, but he was anything but. Of all the most talented players I ever played with, I would pick Charlie up front for his vision and touch and at the back it would be Toddy and McFarland, who were awesome.

'Apart from missing a couple of games after getting sent off against Man United I hardly missed a game in my time at Derby. I think I improved in my second full season, and part of that was because when I went home to Ireland in the summer of 1977 I did some special training to build myself up, to make me stronger and more competitive. Those body exercises are probably the reason for the way I am now, but never mind. I enjoyed that season.'

Dave was also appreciative of his treatment by Tommy Docherty. 'The Doc liked Irish people – I don't know why – and I never had any problems with him. He liked to have a laugh, and I never saw him in a bad mood. But I don't think we saw him at his best, and the team of course went downhill. Then Colin Addison came in, and he was another nice guy and an enthusiastic coach, very approachable, but he took over a side that was in decline, and he can't be blamed for what happened.'

The slide was seemingly inexorable. The Rams escaped relegation by the skin of their teeth in Docherty's final season in charge, 1978–79, but as Liverpool took their fourth title in five years in the campaign that followed, Addison, despite making David Swindlehurst Derby's first £400,000 player, could do nothing to prevent the Rams being doomed to relegation with Bolton Wanderers and Bristol City. The top-flight adventure begun by Brian Clough was over after 11 seasons.

The popular Langan had played the last of his 155 games for the Rams and was off-loaded for £350,000 to Birmingham City, whose manager Jim Smith broke the West Midlands club's transfer record to get his man. 'I didn't know anything about the interest from Birmingham until Colin Addison phoned me and asked me if I wanted to go,' says Dave. 'I asked him what he thought, and he said he didn't want me to leave but the club needed the money, so I went to speak to Jim Smith and that was the end of my Derby days.'

He won the first of 26 caps for the Republic of Ireland – against Turkey in April 1978 – while still a Derby player and was a regular in the squad until he sustained a knee injury in a famous 3–2 victory over France. Though his club and international career was disrupted by a serious injury during his Birmingham days – he was out of the game for 18 months – Jim Smith, by then managing Oxford United, gave him another chance, and Dave returned to top form, regaining his international place and playing an important part in the qualifying matches for Euro '88. His favourite recollection of wearing the green shirt of Ireland is playing against Maradona. 'I wouldn't change that for anything, despite what has happened to me,' he says. 'I got Man of the Match against Maradona, but he was awesome, such a low centre of gravity and amazing balance; unbelievable. They just told me to go man-for-man on him, and that's what I did. Every time he got the ball I was on him like a shot, and I tried to stop the ball getting to him. Somehow during that match, I actually flicked the ball over Maradona's head, and someone has voted that the most memorable moment in Irish football!'

Dave played 136 games for Oxford, winning the Second Division Championship in 1984–85 and the League Cup the following year, and later played for AFC Bournemouth and Peterborough United before knee and back injuries ended his career. In late 2006, a newspaper interview with the unlucky Langan inspired Ireland fans to start campaigning to get him a testimonial. This campaign picked up

David Langan gets the ball across against Chelsea at the Baseball Ground in October 1978, despite the efforts of Ray Lewington. The Rams won 1–0 through an own-goal by Ron Harris.

momentum early in 2008 when an online petition was supported by thousands of signatures, many of them Derby County fans.

'I had two magnificent seasons at Oxford,' says Dave, 'but I suppose Derby has to be my best years because of the great players who were my teammates and because I won Player of the Year in 1977–78, so that would be the greatest season for me.'

However, did he, I wondered, recall those uncomfortable acknowledgements when Rams fans chanted his name before kick-off? 'You bet! I was a very shy guy, and when they called my name I was so scared to put my hand up. The worst thing was when photographers came on before kick-off to take your photo – I hated that. I was very nervous about anything like that and still am today.'

That such a fine professional still carries the scars of his footballing career is heart-breaking, but Dave Langan gets on with his life as best he can. 'I have a very simple job at Peterborough Town Hall,' he says. 'There's no heavy lifting. I just look after people, pouring coffees and teas, but unfortunately I can't do much more than that because my knees and back are shot. It's been quite a struggle, and it would be nice if the testimonial happened.

'That said, I wouldn't change my football career for anything. I hear the Derby supporters are backing the petition, and to me they were the best, because Derby is a football city and they were very good to me.'

1978–79 **Steve Powell**

There's a lovely story, which I had always assumed was too good to be true, about Steve Powell's Rams debut exactly a month after his 16th birthday. It goes like this: Young Powell, still an apprentice, is called into the first team by Brian Clough for a Texaco Cup match at the Baseball Ground. He is a sensation and, possibly because he is the current skipper of England Schoolboys, manages to give the impression he is actually in charge of a Rams side featuring established stars such as McFarland, Todd and Hector.

At one point the ball runs into touch and as Terry Hennessey, 13 years Powell's senior, prepares to take a throw-in, the youngster barks: 'Leave it to me son!' Hennessey, bewildered, dutifully throws the ball to Powell and a new star is born.

'It's true – I said that to Terry,' Steve laughs. 'When you're that age you have no fear. Back then I just wanted to play football.'

While the 3–2 Texaco Cup victory over Stoke City in October 1971 was insignificant in terms of Derby County's mighty achievements in a memorable decade, Steve's contribution to the crucial last game of that 1971–72 season was anything but.

I had the privilege to interview Steve's dad Tommy – a Rams legend in his own right – in 1996, a couple of years before his death, and he described a phone call from the great Clough on the day of that famous Championship-deciding match. 'I was working at the *Derby Telegraph* at the time,' Tommy told me, 'and Cloughie called and said, "Your bairn's in the team against Liverpool tonight. He's fast asleep right now, but he'll be fine". I couldn't believe it!'

Steve recalls: 'In those days we trained on the morning of an evening match, had lunch at the Midland Hotel and slept in the afternoon. It was our last game, Liverpool had one in hand and we had to beat them to stand any chance of winning the title. Eventually we pipped Leeds and Liverpool by a single point, but to me it was just another game. It didn't hit home that football in Derby had changed forever until the following season when as champions of England we were playing in Europe.'

Steve Powell – known to his Derby teammates as 'Rocker'.

In his *Derby Evening Telegraph* match report Gerald Mortimer had no doubts about Steve's impact on the historic 1–0 win over Liverpool: 'Derby's composure did not suffer a whit by the presence of Steve Powell in place of the injured Webster,' Mortimer wrote. 'Powell was brilliant. Not brilliant for a 16-year-old: just brilliant. Other players gave him the ball with confidence, and he did not let them down. Such is his skill that anyone can pick him out now as a future England player...'

In the history of Derby County there has never been a family quite like the Powells. Tommy played 406 games for the Rams between 1948 and 1961 and Steve just beat him with 420 between 1971 and 1985. It never occurred to either of them to play for anyone else. Both were Derby born, educated at Bemrose School; one-club men.

Steve Powell in September 1979.

'I saw my dad play once when I was about seven,' says Steve. 'But it's a vague memory. Obviously there was a family tradition there, but he never pushed me. Football was just something I wanted to do.'

Despite his heroic last-match performance, Steve did not play enough games to get a Championship-winners' medal in 1971–72. His League debut had come as a substitute in a 2–1 home win over Arsenal three days after the Stoke Texaco Cup game, while his full League debut was a 2–0 win at Forest. 'Even for a local lad, the Forest match didn't mean as much as some people might think, because back then there wasn't the local rivalry that seems to have developed in recent years,' Steve explains. 'The big match was definitely Derby versus Leeds because of the feeling between the two managers, Brian Clough and Don Revie.'

Of Clough, Steve says: 'I had a great relationship with him. I remember the little things he did. If you hadn't played too well he'd surprise you with praise, saying something like, "You're the first name on my team sheet son". Then, when you had done well, he'd pick you up on something, I suppose to keep your feet on the ground.'

Steve did not have to wait long to get a Championship medal, as the Rams, now managed by Dave Mackay, won the title again in 1974–75. 'Dave was a great manager in his own way. He brought in some tremendous players, and the high point for me was the Easter period when we won three out of three against Luton, Burnley and Manchester City. That really set us up for the title.'

The following season was looking even better for the Rams. Mackay had nicked Charlie George from Arsenal, and at the start of April 1976 his entertaining side was still in the hunt for a League

Steve Powell and Viv Anderson clash at the Baseball Ground in April 1979. Derby lost 2–1 to Forest that day.

and FA Cup double. 'There's no doubt that Charlie dislocating his shoulder before the FA Cup semi-final against Manchester United messed up our chances,' says Steve, who played in the 2–0 defeat at Hillsborough. 'It's fair to say things went downhill after that.'

So much so that Steve would see a succession of managers in his time at Derby. 'Nine bosses in total – it's like a pub quiz question!' Steve jokes. 'They came and went, but it didn't really bother me. I took the view that my job was to play football – that's what I got paid for. If I didn't particularly get on with a manager it didn't make much difference. To my mind, it's the supporters you play for, and I always tried to perform.'

So the slide continued, with Steve battling on regardless as the Baseball Ground hot seat was transferred like a hot potato from Mackay to Murphy and on to Docherty, Addison, Newman, Taylor, McFarland and, finally, Cox.

Steve Powell appears to get the better of Aston Villa's Ken McNaught at Villa Park in March 1980, but the Rams eventually lost 1–0.

Dubbed 'The Rocker' by teammate David Langan because of his long hair, Steve was the type of player who passed the ball with vision and often brought a collective wince from the crowd for his full-blooded challenges. It was almost inevitable injuries would take a toll. 'It was sad from my career point of view that we went from the top flight to the Third Division,' Steve admits, 'but it was harder for the fans because they had seen fantastic times.'

Despite being labelled at 16 the 'young player most likely to make it big', full international honours eluded Steve. 'I have no regrets. It was a fantastic honour to represent my country at schoolboy, youth and Under-23 level, and it was up to whoever was managing England at the time to decide whether I was good enough.'

Player of the Year in 1978–79 when he missed only one League game as Docherty's side battled in the wrong half of the First Division, Steve is emphatic on the one-club question. 'I know a couple of clubs came in for me, but why would I want to leave my home club?' he says. 'I was happy in Derby, and I still am.'

He limped off the Baseball Ground pitch for the last time after a 4–1 Third Division victory over Reading in April 1985. 'I'd picked up a chronic knee injury some years before and was living on borrowed time. I had to finish, but I count myself lucky to have been part of the club at a time when it created a buzz around the whole city. Let's hope that can happen again.'

Manager at the fitness centre at Derby College for well over a decade, Steve has two sons, Stevie and David, and there were hopes at one time that Stevie, a former Rams apprentice, would become the third generation of Powells to make it at Derby County. 'He played a couple of times for the reserves and did well,' says Steve. 'I'm sure he could have made a career of it, but the main thing is he's a smashing lad and he's doing well in his career.'

Whisper it, but Steve now has a grandson, Josh Powell, born to this amazing football family a couple of years ago. 'I already had a granddaughter, but Josh is my first grandson,' smiles Steve, 'so, who knows...?'

1979–80 & 1981–82 **Steve Buckley**

There is a photograph of Roger Davies diving in to head one of his five goals in the demolition of Luton Town at the Baseball Ground in March 1975 as the Rams marched to their second Championship. Big Roger became the first Derby player to achieve five goals in a match since Hughie Gallacher did it at Blackburn 41 years earlier, and one of the Luton players on that photograph, watching helplessly as yet another one hit the back of the net, is the 21-year-old Steve Buckley.

So superior were the Rams that day, Roger also had two goals disallowed, and in the dying minutes Buckley cleared Davies's goal-bound header off the line as the striker went for a sixth. 'All I can remember about that game is we got absolutely murdered,' Steve tells me. 'Derby were a really top team at that time and Luton were struggling. We got a right hammering!'

Three years later 'Bucko' was a Derby County player, the only Tommy Docherty signing to become a long-term hit with Rams supporters. So much so, he was the first player to win the Jack Stamps Trophy on two occasions – in 1980 and 1982 – a record equalled by only one other player, Mark Wright.

For more than eight years and under five managers he was a fixture in the team and set a remarkable club record as the only player to complete two separate centuries of consecutive League appearances.

Born on the Notts-Derbyshire border in Eastwood, Steve came from a footballing family. 'I would say we were mostly Forest when I was growing up, both me and our Alan and my dad, but on alternate weeks we'd go to watch Notts County when Forest were away. We'd just want to watch football,' he says. His older brother Alan was already a prolific striker at Walsall as Steve, once an apprentice at

Steve Buckley (far left) lines up a free-kick in the 1–1 draw with Blackburn Rovers at the Baseball Ground in October 1981.

Nottingham Forest, played non-League football on the Rams' doorstep with Ilkeston Town and then Burton Albion.

Steve was also a forward before being converted to left-back during his time with the Brewers, though this did not stop him eventually rattling in 25 goals – many of them breathtaking efforts – in 366 games for the Rams. 'I'd always played centre-forward and up front from primary school until I went to Burton Albion, but I was eventually persuaded it was easier to play at the back than it was up front – but I never lost the desire to score goals,' he says.

However, it was Luton Town and not Derby County that spotted Buckley's potential, signing him from Burton in April 1974 as the Hatters clinched promotion to the First Division, where they would stay for only a single season, despite beating Derby 1–0 at Kenilworth Road four days before Christmas 1974. It was a game in which Buckley played so well the travelling supporters were prompted to wonder how on earth he had slipped through the Rams' scouting net. 'I had trials at Forest and at Derby, but they obviously thought I wasn't good enough so I had to get a job,' Steve recalls.

Steve Buckley (right) is a happy man. He has just scored in the Rams' 2–1 win over Wrexham at the Baseball Ground in November 1981.

By the time Derby were ready to pounce, they had to pay £163,000 for his services, but it was still money well spent. When David Nish limped out of a 1–0 home win over Bristol City on 17 December 1977 it meant yet another operation on a right knee he had first injured in the process of scoring a goal against Sheffield United exactly two years before. One of the most elegant defenders to wear a Derby shirt, Nish's career was now effectively over at the age of 30, and manager Docherty needed a replacement. The ever-willing Peter Daniel filled in at left-back for a few games until Bucko arrived to make his Derby debut in a classic Baseball Ground encounter against Forest, the club he had supported as a kid. 'Tommy Docherty was a real comedian, a bubbly character, and at his peak I imagine he was a fantastic manager to play for,' says Steve. 'By the time he came to Derby he probably wasn't so driven, but he was still good to play for.

'That first match was a big game for me. At Luton I'd be lucky to play in front of 10,000 and suddenly I was in the team against Forest with a sell-out at the Baseball Ground of something like 33,000. I was playing with world-class players, and having come from Luton I did often think "What am I doing with this lot?". But I managed to adjust quite well, and of course Roy and Toddy were brilliant to play with at the back.'

A little over four years since Brian Clough and Peter Taylor had left Derby County they were back at the Baseball Ground. After winning promotion the previous May, Clough and Taylor had taken the

First Division by storm once again, and Forest were top of the table going into the local derby game on 14 January 1978. Forest's impact had been apparent as early as the third match of the season when Colin Murphy, who would be in charge for only four more games before making way for The Doc, had seen his Derby side beaten easily 3–0 at the City Ground. By the end of the 1977–78 campaign Clough had clinched his second League title.

On this occasion, however, Forest had to share the points and had the matchless Peter Shilton to thank for keeping them in the game. It ended goalless, but Buckley, playing superbly on debut, demonstrated in the second half what a valuable signing he would become when, after Derby's defence had been caught out by a quick throw-in, he chased back to tackle Forest's Peter Withe as the striker prepared to shoot at John Middleton's goal.

The draw meant Docherty's team had taken 15 points out of a possible 20, and hopes were high of European qualification; however, although this was still the side of McFarland, Todd, Rioch and George, a 4–0 thrashing on The Doc's return to Old Trafford was just seven days away, and Derby would record only five wins from the last 17 games of the season, finishing 12th. One of those victories in an inconsistent run-in was a 4–1 home win over a Leicester City side doomed to relegation in which Buckley drove home his first Derby goal in a match dominated by the brilliance of Charlie George, who scored two that day and had a hand in all four.

For Bucko, it was the start of a long journey. He was an ever present from the day of his debut until 117 League games later when he missed his first match on 12 November 1980, with a groin injury, by which time both Docherty and the First Division were things of the past, and Steve was the reigning Player of the Year for the first time. Commenting on his remarkable appearance record, Steve says 'I think everyone played with injuries in those days. I rarely missed training, and I had two relatively injury-free spells. I think these days the game has altered. It's a lot faster, and maybe that's why players seem to get far more injuries.'

The fans had appreciated the honest endeavours of the dependable left-back in the relegation campaign of 1979–80, voting him the Jack Stamps Trophy winner. Docherty had resigned after a

Steve Buckley scores from the penalty spot in the 1–0 win against Chelsea at the Baseball Ground in September 1982.

From left to right: Steve Buckley, Ross MacLaren and Rob Hindmarch, celebrate on a rainy night in May 1986 when the Rams beat Rotherham United 2–1 at the Baseball Ground to seal promotion to Division Two.

19th-place top-flight finish in Steve's first full season and new boss Colin Addison, despite signing David Swindlehurst, Alan Biley and Barry Powell, could do nothing to stop the rot that had seemed to set in at Hillsborough in the FA Cup semi-final defeat in the spring of 1976.

Buckley was Player of the Year again in another difficult season, 1981–82, as Addison and then John Newman struggled to keep Derby afloat in the old Second Division. Bucko played a couple of games in midfield at the start of that campaign before reverting to his familiar number-three shirt for the visit of Leicester City on 12 September, and the Baseball Ground crowd were treated to a Bucko 'special'. Kevin Hector, who also scored in a 3–1 win, was tripped just outside the box, and when the free-kick was tapped to Buckley he let fly with a left-foot screamer that Mark Wallington could only admire as it flew past him into the net. Not even a young Leicester substitute by the name of Gary Lineker could inspire his side that afternoon.

Survival was still not guaranteed as Watford visited the Baseball Ground for the last game of that 1981–82 season, and although the two-time recipient of the Jack Stamps Trophy hit another stunning goal that afternoon, the headlines were stolen by the 37-year-old Hector, who typically signed off from his historic Derby County career by heading the winner. Earlier Buckley had bent a magnificent shot into the far top corner of the net to give a nervous Rams side a much-needed lift.

A year later he broke his leg going in bravely for a loose ball with Charlton Athletic's Mark Aizlewood in a night match at the Baseball Ground. Aizlewood was booked, and Buckley missed the six remaining matches of the season.

Derby made a dreadful start to the 1983–84 relegation season with a 5–0 defeat at Chelsea's Stamford Bridge, where Buckley was substituted before being placed on the transfer list by Peter Taylor. 'The broken leg was one thing, but the bigger problem was that I came back too early trying to prove a point because everyone was saying I was finished,' says Steve. 'I pulled my thigh and was out longer with that than I was with the broken leg. Peter Taylor put me on the list I think through frustration. I don't know if he thought I was trying to pull a fast one, but he only had to look at my record to see what type of person I was.'

A lesser man would have capitulated; instead Buckley fought, earning a recall to the side for a 1–0 win at Cambridge on 5 November 1983, and never missed another League game – 122 in all – before bowing out at Darlington on 12 May 1986, as the Rams, promoted from the Third Division three days earlier thanks to victory over Rotherham United, ended that campaign with a 2–1 defeat. It was a phenomenal achievement. Including Cup games, the appearance sequence actually extended to 144 games, although Bucko did miss the Southern qualifying group match at Brentford in the Freight Rover Trophy in January 1986…but who's counting?

Released by Arthur Cox in the summer of 1986, Bucko joined Lincoln City and finished his playing career at Boston United and Eastwood Town. 'I had a clause in my contract that automatically gave me an extra year at Derby in the event of us getting promoted in 1986, and of course we did,' says Steve. 'But I'd had a few problems with my back and was struggling at times despite not missing a game, and I think Arthur decided I wasn't going to play a full season again. I was still pretty fit except for my back.'

In a period of decline, Steve Buckley was a shining light, and whatever the match and whatever the division (he played in three for Derby) Rams supporters knew they could be assured unstinting commitment from one of the club's great servants. 'We had a couple of relegations, but playing at Derby at the Baseball Ground was always a fantastic experience in that atmosphere. There was talk throughout my career about me one day going to Forest, but I don't regret staying at Derby. It meant a lot to be Player of the Year twice. I had a good rapport with the fans, and they were always very fair to me.

'The only football I see these days is on TV and watching my son play for Long Eaton Under-16s. Thomas is a left-back, all left-footed, and if it's possible I think he's even more left-footed than me!'

1980–81 **Roger Jones**

It was hardly an auspicious start to his Derby career as goalkeeper Roger Jones conceded three goals on his Rams debut at Cambridge United on 16 August 1980, when the grim reality of life in the Second Division began to hit home.

The Rams, twice officially the best club in England in the 1970s and used to mixing it with the best in the world, were now second best at the unassuming Abbey Stadium. In their first season out of the top flight since 1969, Derby fielded only two players – Roy McFarland and Steve Powell – associated with the glory days. Also playing in front of Jones that day were Steve Emery, Steve Buckley, Alan Ramage, Jon Clark, Barry Powell, Alan Biley, Dave Swindlehurst and Paul Emson. The halcyon days were indeed at an end.

Although possibly at fault for one of the Cambridge goals, Jones at least emerged from an embarrassing game with some credit. The Derby goal was under such intense pressure that the 'keeper was often forced to rescue his defence, despite the presence of the vastly experienced McFarland, who in season 1980–81 became the seventh Rams player to complete 500 appearances before being released at the end of the campaign to become player-manager at Bradford City.

Roger Jones.

Manager Colin Addison delivered a collective slap to his players, who recorded victories in the next three League games against Chelsea, Luton Town and Bolton Wanderers.

While Derby's Mr Consistency Steve Buckley finally gave way to injury in the November of 1980 to end a remarkable run of 127 first-team appearances, in goal Jones was taking on the mantle of the team's most reliable player.

Already a veteran at 33 when he signed for the Rams from Stoke City in the summer of 1980, Jones had started his career as an apprentice at Portsmouth, moving along the South Coast to Bournemouth before playing for six seasons between 1970 and 1976 at Blackburn Rovers during dark days for the Lancashire club in the Second and Third Divisions. He was good enough, though, to win England Under-23 recognition and briefly followed Rovers manager Gordon Lee to Newcastle. His transfer to the St James'

Jones clears his lines.

Park club caused a huge row when Newcastle refused to pay Blackburn a fee because of apparent medical problems. Jones confounded the experts, however, and went on to play just short of 300 more League games for Stoke, whom he joined in February 1977, before signing for Derby and finally York City, where he was voted the best 'keeper in the club's history.

Before Jones's arrival at the Baseball Ground, the goalkeeping duties had been shared by David McKellar and John Middleton, the first of three former Forest 'keepers who would go on to play for the Rams (Peter Shilton and Steve Sutton are the other two). Also straining at the leash was young 'keeper Steve Cherry, an apprentice at Derby since 1978. The unfortunate Middleton, whose career was curtailed by injury and illness, will always be remembered as the player Tommy Docherty agreed to exchange with a gleeful Brian Clough for Archie Gemmill. Although then 31, the Scottish midfielder had plenty of football left in his legs. Unfortunately for Derby, Middleton did not.

Jones was brought in as number one, and that's the position he held throughout 1980–81, never missing a League or Cup game and keeping 14 clean sheets along the way. Immaculate when put under pressure

Former Derby goalkeeper Roger Jones is beaten by Bobby Davison who scores after only two minutes of the Rams' 1–1 draw with York City at Bootham Crescent in April 1985.

from high crosses into his penalty area, Jones was a reassuring presence throughout a season that saw the surprise return of Kevin Hector from non-League football. Fourteen years after first arriving at the Baseball Ground, 'The King' was back to accumulate more games than any other Derby player as he passed the appearance record set by Ron Webster.

For Jones, who played 46 games (next came Steve Powell and Emson, both with 36 appearances), the season ended in unfortunate fashion. Presented with the Jack Stamps Trophy before the last game kicked-off at the Baseball Ground against lowly Preston, the goalkeeper could do nothing to prevent the visitors' striker Alex Bruce giving his side the lead in the 72nd minute. Although Swindlehurst equalised soon afterwards, Jones, so reliable all season, uncharacteristically failed to deal with a cross and, in the process of trying to punch the ball managed to dislocate a finger. Bruce was left to poke the loose ball into an empty net and Jones, complaining he had been fouled, had to leave the field, with Steve Buckley finishing the game in goal.

Still, Addison's side had finished sixth behind the three promoted clubs, Swansea, Notts County and champions West Ham. Although he started the 1981–82 campaign as number one, Jones's unbroken run in the side came to an end six games into that season when he picked up a groin injury. Cherry deputised for four games, but Jones returned

Jones, immaculate on crosses.

when fit again to play his part in another season of struggle that saw Addison replaced by his assistant John Newman in the new year of 1982.

Newman's first match in charge was at Watford on 26 January. It was to be Jones's last as the Hornets, managed by Graham Taylor, boosted by chairman Elton John's cash and boasting a forward line that included John Barnes and Luther Blissett, hit Derby for six. Following that humiliating 6–1 defeat, Jones was loaned out to Birmingham City to be replaced in the Derby goal by the Yugoslavian Vjekoslav Banovic, signed by Addison the previous September. Jones was sold to York City in the summer of 1982, where he stayed for six years before coaching under former teammate Denis Smith, looking after the reserves and youngsters at Sunderland.

Later he became assistant manager when Malcolm Crosby, a future Derby County first-team coach, took charge, but he eventually dropped out of the game to run a painting and decorating business.

1982–83 **Steve Cherry**

There was something of the old and the new about the Rams' early-season encounter with Queen's Park Rangers back in 1981. The legendary Kevin Hector – in his second spell with the club and by now a wily player rather than the billy whizz of his youth – scored twice in a 3–1 home victory that September day. The 36-year-old Hector was well on his way to an all-time record number of Derby County appearances and cracking the 200-mark for Rams goals. At the other end of the spectrum, in goal against a QPR side that featured a future Rams player and manager John Gregory, was Steve Cherry, just turned 21 and playing his sixth game for a club he had joined as a kid.

Just over 11,000 fans turned out at the Baseball Ground to watch a home team featuring the likes of Mick Coop, Barry Powell and young Frank Gamble, making his first appearance in a Derby County career that stuttered to a halt at seven. QPR, managed by Terry Venables, were altogether more star-studded, with Tony Currie strutting his stuff in midfield, Terry Fenwick and Glenn Roeder at the back and Gregory, who scored the visitors' goal that day.

Significantly – and this emphasises that, for goalkeepers in particular, patience is a precious commodity – it was Cherry's first appearance at the Baseball Ground in 16 months. Still a teenager and playing third fiddle in Colin Addison's squad of 1979–80 to John Middleston and David McKellar, his previous home game had been the penultimate match of that relegation season, a 3–1 win over

Steve Cherry *(back row, far right)* plays for Derby County Masters. The other ex-Rams (back row from left to right) are: Mark Lillis, Roger Davies, Andy Garner, Dick Pratley, Martin Kuhl. *(Front row from left to right) are:* David Penney, David Preece, Phil Gee, Steve Cross and Gary Micklewhite.

Bryan Robson and Norman Whiteside close in on goal as Steve Cherry makes a flying save in Manchester United's 1–0 win in the FA Cup fifth round at the Baseball Ground in February 1983.

Manchester City. It was not enough to save the Rams from slipping out of the top flight and the young 'keeper conceded four in the last game of the campaign at Norwich.

Roger Jones arrived the following season, and no other 'keeper got a look-in as the 1980–81 Player of the Year started and finished every single game before finally succumbing to injury after five games of the new 1981–82 season. So Cherry stepped out of the shadows for a 2–0 defeat at Bolton on 23 September and three days later was able to sample first-team life again at the Baseball Ground. 'I don't honestly remember anything about that game,' Steve tells me. 'There are some stand-out matches from my time at Derby, and I still have a few videos that remind me of some of my performances in a Derby shirt, but most of it is just a blur.'

Despite his roots on the wrong side of the A52, Steve had no particular club allegiance as a youngster. 'Believe it or not I never watched a live game of football as a kid,' he says. 'All I wanted to do was play football. I was on the verge of getting a trial with Notts County when a Derby scout came to watch me play for my youth team. We got hammered 7–0, but I actually had a blinding game and was offered schoolboy forms at the Baseball Ground.

'When I arrived at Derby the squad was incredible, full of big names like McFarland, Todd, Hector, Lee and Charlie George. To work with those guys in training was amazing.'

The highlight of the season was undoubtedly the FA Cup third-round home victory over high-flying Nottingham Forest. On any other day the Rams taking on their biggest rivals at the Baseball Ground would have been big enough, but this was even bigger. Not just Derby versus Forest, it was Taylor versus Clough; two former best mates who had fallen out big style.

Steve Cherry punches clear in the controversial game at the Baseball Ground in May 1983. Derby won 1–0 to stay up, but Fulham wanted the game replayed after a crowd invasion cut it short by 78 seconds. Other Rams players are Wilson, Burns, Futcher and Hooks.

A crowd of 28,494 watched in astonishment as Derby County, struggling in 22nd place in Division Two, not only beat Forest – sitting pretty in fourth spot in the top tier of English football – they played them off the park. 'Yes, I remember that one!' says Steve. 'It is the only night I can remember in my local village where there wasn't a single Forest fan to be seen! The big memory is Archie Gemmill's free-kick past Steve Sutton. I remember Archie running around like a spring kitchen celebrating the goal – no one could catch him!'

While the Forest game was a significant FA Cup memory for Steve, another was to come the following season – his last with the Rams. It is something of an irritation that the sixth-round replay defeat to Plymouth Argyle would blight his Derby County career. This time the Rams were the hot favourites to progress into the semi-finals of the FA Cup against lower League opposition. But their Wembley dreams were left in ruins by a freak goal scored direct from a corner by Alan Rogers.

In truth, the entire team played badly. Plymouth were the better side, hitting the woodwork twice, with manager Taylor hardly helping matters by replacing top scorer Bobby Davison with old warhorse Dave Watson – a central-defender – with 20 minutes to play.

The Rams, facing winding-up petitions in the High Court from Inland Revenue and Customs and Excise, had been informed that same day that a reported rescue bid from media magnate Robert Maxwell was off. 'I do get a bit annoyed when people forever go on about that goal,' says Steve. 'What seems to have been forgotten is that Plymouth battered us at their place and I had the game of my life to keep us in the tie. In the first place we shouldn't have conceded the corner. I remember shouting to John Barton to knock it long, but he put it behind. When the ball came over I admit I was put off by Tommy Tynan coming in at pace, but even with me missing it we should have had a man on the back post. As it was the ball hit the post and went in. I certainly learned from that mistake.

'Dave Watson had a volley from two yards out and put it straight into their 'keeper's hands, so I know it wasn't all down to me. I have peace of mind. What really disappointed me was that Taylor then dropped me for three games. As a former 'keeper himself he should have known better, but as soon as he got sacked Roy McFarland put me back in.'

Though Maxwell did eventually do enough to save the club from oblivion, these were dark days indeed. Relegated to the Third Division just nine years after winning the First Division title, Derby County were in a mess, and it was a sad time for Steve. After chalking up 90 appearances, he left a club that had given him his first chance in the game. 'Looking back, moving on was a mistake,' Steve admits. 'I was irritated that having seen off the likes of John Middleton, Dave McKellar and Banovic, all of whom came in on bigger money than me, I wasn't offered a better contract. There was a three-year offer on the table, and I can admit now that I should have taken it.

'Arthur Cox was appointed in the summer of 1984, and he called me into his office and said he'd seen me play brilliant, average and poor, but he wanted me to stay and improve. Being naïve, I went to Walsall, and it was the wrong move.'

After Walsall, Steve went on to play in the colours of Chesterfield, Notts County, Watford, Plymouth, Rotherham, Kettering, Rushden & Diamonds, Stalybridge Celtic, Mansfield Town, Oldham Athletic, Lincoln City, Kidsgrove Athletic, Belper Town and Spalding United before becoming part-time goalkeeping coach in the summer of 2006 at Notts County, the club with whom he enjoyed most success.

'I left Derby at 24 and as a goalkeeper that's still incredibly young,' he says. 'I improved a lot after that, particularly in terms of commanding my box. Like every young 'keeper I took my knocks and

Steve receives a memento of his Player of the Year award from Peter Taylor in 1983. The Jack Stamps Trophy always remained in the club's possession.

Steve Cherry in action against Plymouth on 10 March 1984.

came back. Ironically, my home debut for Plymouth was against Derby, and I was voted Man of the Match, and down the years whenever I played against the Rams I enjoyed a strange banter with Derby's fans. That never bothered me. Rather than getting rattled I was always lifted by the things they chanted.'

Signed by Neil Warnock, Steve joined Notts County in February 1989 and became a huge fans' favourite as the Magpies went from the old Division Three to Division One. He played 170 consecutive games, finally missing a game three matches into the 1992–93 season, but was soon back and started all but one of Notts' games in 1993–94 when they were losers at Wembley in the Anglo-Italian Cup against Brescia. Steve eventually claimed a winners' medal in the same competition the following year – his last at Meadow Lane as a player – when Notts beat Ascoli 2–1. He made 328 appearances for the Magpies.

'Looking back, in addition to the Forest Cup game one of my favourite Derby games was the fifth-round home match that same season against Manchester United,' he says. 'I had a good game that day, and we were on the brink of taking United to a replay at Old Trafford when Norman Whiteside finally got one past me with five minutes to go.

'I will always be grateful for my time at Derby because not only did I make loads of friends in the game, the feedback from the fans was fantastic. I used to spend a lot of time at different supporters' club events, so much so I used to get into trouble at home! It was simply because they were such a great bunch of people.'

1983–84 **Archie Gemmill**

It is a sunny September day and Archie Gemmill is sitting outside an executive box against the backdrop of a plush early-season Pride Park pitch. He studies me with the same narrow-eyed suspicion with which he once viewed midfield opponents, the likes of Billy Bremner and Tommy Smith, across the Baseball Ground battlefield.

Okay, so he's at least a foot shorter than Peter Crouch, but there's no doubting Archie is a big man who should not be messed with. 'Growing up in Paisley I never felt the need to prove anything just because I was small,' he tells me. 'I've always had a bit of devilment about me and got into scrapes for saying too much, even as a kid.'

Then he smiles. 'The trick was to get friendly with the biggest lads at school. That way, whenever I got into trouble, I would refer whoever it was to my big mate!'

Like just about every other kid growing up in a Glasgow suburb around 50 years ago, Archie played football at play time, at dinner time and after school until it was too dark to see from one makeshift street 'goal' to the other. 'That's the way it was in those days, and it's sad today's youngsters spend so much time indoors because street football was how a lot of talent was nurtured,' says Archie. 'My first organised matches were with the Boys' Brigade. I did reasonably well and signed on with St Mirren at 16. I had the chance to go to Rangers or Celtic, but my parents thought it would be better to try to make it at a smaller club. They were probably right. I made my debut at 17 and won the Player of the Year award that same year. That's how I got started.'

Two broken legs hampered progress in his second season, but young Archie had done enough to grab the attention of a Preston scout named Jimmy Scott. 'The Preston move came out of the blue,' he says, 'and being an only child (I was spoiled rotten and probably cried every time I didn't get my own way!) I asked my parents what I should do. They told me it was too good an opportunity to turn down. I think they realised I was ready for a new way of life. I was, and still am to an extent, a bit insular. I like my own company, and they thought it would be good for me.

Archie Gemmill (1970–1977 and 1982–1984).

Archie Gemmill with the Football League Championship trophy on 26 April 1975.

'I enjoyed my time at Preston because there was a good group of Scottish players who mixed well socially, and I made some life-long friends.'

Archie's engine – the incredible fitness that supported his non-stop, buzzing style – soon brought him to the attention of the English game's reigning champions Everton, and the loudmouthed young manager of newly-promoted Derby County. Preston's manager Alan Ball Snr, the father of the World Cup winner of the same name who by then was playing for Everton, had more or less agreed the deal with Everton's Harry Catterick 'It was a three-year contract, which suited me because Goodison Park was only a 40-minute drive from my home in Lytham, which I loved, and my wages were going up astronomically compared with what I was used to.

'The strange thing was that, although Alan Ball was determined I was going to be sold to Everton, he was fascinated by Brian Clough and wanted to meet him. It happened at a hotel in Blackburn. I was there with Alan Ball senior, and he turned up with Stuart Webb and Peter Taylor. As soon as I shook his hand I felt he had an aura about him, something very few people have.'

To this day, Archie still refers to Brian Clough as 'the boss'. It is like nothing will ever impact on the mentor-student relationship forged in those early days, not even the great man's passing in the autumn of 2004.

Clough's strategy to win over Archie was to persuade him that while he did not stand a chance of displacing any player in the Toffees' famed midfield trio of Kendall, Harvey and Ball Jr, he would be a

Skipper Gemmill celebrates the League title win in 1975.

top player at the Baseball Ground. 'It was supposed to be a quiet chat but the boss kept chipping away about not getting a kick if I went to Everton. He would put me straight in the team at Derby, and we would win the Championship. It got late, and Alan Ball Snr was getting worried, so he gave me a nod. We went to the gents and just as Alan was asking, "You are still going to Everton aren't you..?" Peter Taylor appeared between us at the urinals and said "No, he's coming to Derby!"'

The next stage in the wooing of wee Archie is a legendary Clough moment; and perfectly true. Old Big 'Ead followed Archie home and announced he was going nowhere until he had his signature, even if it meant sleeping the night in his car. 'We had a couple of spare rooms so I invited him in,' says Archie. 'My wife Betty cooked him some breakfast in the morning, and afterwards he got the transfer papers out and said "Get them signed!" I did what I was told and took them to Preston. Alan Ball wasn't too happy of course, but I collected my boots and left.'

Despite his extraordinary efforts in getting Archie to Derby (he paid Preston £60,000 for the privilege) Clough soon asserted his authority over his new signing. 'Things didn't start too well,' Archie recalls. 'We lost 2–1 at West Brom in my first game, and I wasn't settling in particularly well. It's not that the top flight was too fast for me – I could get around the pitch okay – I just needed to use my head a bit more.'

A dressing room bust-up changed things. 'At that time Alan Hinton was probably the best crosser of a ball in the English game. The problem was we didn't work well together. I kept making forward runs for Ally and he never gave me the ball. So at half-time in one particular match, myself and Ally got into a bit of an argument. The boss just sat back and listened to us for a while and then ended it by turning to me and saying "Right – it's simple. He's a better player than you and if you don't give the ball to him you won't be in my team, so it's your choice."

'Ally was a fantastic player, a bit timid at times, but most wingers are, except perhaps for Mike Summerbee. When I look back over my time at Derby County he must have been involved in 60 per cent of the goals we scored. So, as ever, the boss was absolutely right, and I learned to give Ally the ball at every opportunity.'

That a collection of unexceptional individuals – that was the outside world's perception at any rate – somehow managed to become League champions in Archie's second season was a puzzle to many in the media and even to some Rams fans. 'The winning formula was that we gelled together,' says Archie. 'We had a terrific bunch of lads who had great faith in each other's ability. It is fair to say the Derby and Nottingham public never really appreciated John McGovern. They saw him as a gangly lad, but for me he was a fabulous player, and the boss obviously thought the same. I have never played with a better midfielder, certainly not one that balanced so well with me. If I went forward he covered me, and vice-versa. John O'Hare was another underrated player. He couldn't run – that wasn't his forte – but he was terrific to play with.'

A 1–0 victory at Old Trafford in October 1973 was the unlikely starting point for the biggest upheaval in the history of Derby County. Seven days later Brian Clough was waving farewell to Rams fans as the side he created prepared to take on Leicester City at the Baseball Ground. 'We knew something was going off after the Manchester United match, but we never thought it was as serious as it turned out. The boss left behind a team that could only get better, so it was incredibly disappointing.'

Would Clough have achieved the European success he enjoyed at Forest if he'd stayed put? 'The boss would have achieved anything anywhere because he was special,' says Archie. 'Leeds didn't give him a chance of course, but he was a one-off. Football to him was very simple, very basic. You did it his way or you didn't play.

'In every team there are players who, off the pitch, you don't particularly like. But at both Derby and Forest the boss somehow instilled a loyalty in his teams to the extent that, for 90 minutes on the pitch, even those you didn't particularly like were comrades you would die for if necessary.'

Only Dave Mackay – in his last season as a player at the Baseball Ground when Archie arrived – could possibly have filled the vacuum created by Clough's departure. 'Dave was possibly the best player I ever played with,' Archie declares. 'Everyone has a picture in their heads of Dave Mackay the hard man with his sleeves rolled up. What many forget is that he had so much talent and an incredible football brain.

'As manager at Derby he had three great years, turning around a near impossible situation. He brought in his own players, and we

Archie Gemmill pictured in the 1976–1977 season.

Archie's free-kick beats Steve Sutton in the Rams' famous FA Cup third-round victory over Forest in January 1983.

played wonderful attacking football. He signed the likes of Bruce Rioch, Franny Lee, Charlie George and Leighton James – superb footballers. When I hear people arguing players from that team wouldn't survive today I just laugh. They could have played in today's team on one leg!'

With Roy McFarland sidelined by injury for almost the entire 1974–75 campaign, Mackay made Gemmill his skipper – and at the end of the season the Rams were champions again. 'I always tried to give my best on a football pitch. Sometimes it wasn't good enough, but that was never through lack of effort,' says Archie. 'Getting the captaincy was a bit special because you have to lead by example, even when things aren't going well. It's not just a matter of tossing a coin at the start of the match.'

With Charlie George in the side the following season, Derby were playing even better football and at one stage chasing silverware in the League, FA Cup and in Europe. Archie memorably crossed from the left for George to hit a left-foot screamer against Real Madrid at the Baseball Ground, the pick of Charlie's hat-trick in an astounding 4–1 victory over the Spanish champions. 'I definitely scuffed that cross, but you take anything that comes,' Archie laughs. 'It was very disappointing to do so well at home and then get beaten 5–1 in Madrid. A couple of decisions went against us in Spain, but we should have been good enough to hold on to that advantage.'

The home victory over Real Madrid remains one of Archie's favourite Derby County memories. Little did he or any other member of Mackay's flamboyant side realise, the club's steep decline was just around the corner. 'Just before the FA Cup semi-final against Manchester United, Charlie got injured at Stoke,' Archie recalls. 'He was playing unbelievable football and scoring goals for fun, and losing him at such a key time seemed to spring a leak at the club. It started as a slow drip and eventually drained away to nothing.'

Tommy Docherty opened the floodgates, with apparent relish.

'Dave left, and eventually Docherty came in,' says Archie. 'Straight away he told me I was finished. I was too old and couldn't run. So I didn't hang around. I think he had decided he needed a goalkeeper and the one he wanted was Forest's John Middleton. I can only assume he was told by the boss he could have Middleton in exchange for me. By then I had lost a bit of my buzz, but I could pass the ball better. I walked into a completely new club but immediately felt I had been there all my life. The team spirit and the togetherness were terrific.

'In many ways that Forest team was a mirror image of the first Championship-winning side at Derby. The boss played 4–4–2 in both, and for Hinton we had Robertson, and for Durban we had Martin O'Neill. At the back Burns and Lloyd could have been McFarland and Todd. Both teams played good football. The boss's teams were always among the top goalscorers, but also had the least scored against. Defensively everyone worked for each other to keep clean sheets.'

After helping Clough to another League title win and playing a part in every round of a stunning European Cup adventure in 1978–79, Archie was left out of the final starting line up as Forest went

on to lift the trophy with a 1–0 win over Malmo in Munich. 'I was devastated,' says Archie. 'I had words with the boss after the match, but he proved again he was the boss because soon after we reported back for to pre-season training he sold me. Peter Taylor called me into his office and said he didn't care if I had two years left on my contract, Forest had signed Asa Hartford and he was a better player than me. I was going to Birmingham City. End of...'

Three years later Taylor returned cap in hand to make Archie his first signing in a second spell for both of them at the Baseball Ground. 'I had a good time when I came back to Derby,' Archie says. 'There was the 2–0 home win over Forest when I scored from a free-kick, but I had no massive grudge against the boss – it was just nice to win. The bad time of course

Archie with John McGovern, ex-teammates in management at Rotherham United.

was getting beaten by Plymouth in the fifth-round Cup replay. Steve Cherry made a mistake, and after the game Peter Taylor laid into me, telling me I was washed up and that I would never play again. After two or three matches, Pete got me back into his office with Roy (McFarland) and tried to get me playing again, but I refused. It was only when Pete moved on and Roy became manager that I agreed to play again.

'That year we finished getting beaten 3–0 at Shrewsbury. I missed a penalty, and I knew my time was definitely up. I had a year of my contract left, but I wanted to be remembered as someone who could play a bit rather than someone who went on too long. The only good thing about that last season was that I won the Player of the Year trophy. I had strived for that at both Derby and Forest since my first year at St Mirren. I think it was a sympathy vote!'

A spell coaching Forest's successful youth and reserve teams followed, but it was painful for him to witness the decline of Clough at such close quarters. 'All good things come to an end, and seeing the boss on the slide was very sad,' he says.

A spell in management at Rotherham did not work out for Archie ('I wasn't particularly a success, but neither was I an abject failure') but his career as a coach and trusted scout continued to thrive, including scouting for the Scotland national team and working with the Under-19s.

No Archie Gemmill profile is complete without a reference to one of the most celebrated goals in World Cup history – Archie's bewildering dribble past three Dutch defenders that gave the Scots hope in their Group D fixture in 1978. Needing to win by three clear goals to progress, surely an impossible task against one of the best sides in world football, Archie's miraculous 68th-minute strike put the Scots 3–1 ahead. One of those moments that transcends sport, the goal has been re-worked as a dance movement, a song and even plays a leading role in the film *Trainspotting*, starring Ewan McGregor.

Asked about *that* goal, Archie's response is well-rehearsed – but I could not help thinking that he wants to scream to the world that his career would have still been special even if at the end of that incredible run he had ballooned his final shot high over Jan Jongbloed's bar. What he actually says is: 'I am very delighted it has given so many people so much pleasure. It happened so many years ago yet even on a recent trip to Scotland I had kids of nine and 10 coming up to me saying they'd seen my goal on telly. It only took a matter of seconds to score the goal, and when it went in all I could think of was that we only had to get one more goal to be in the second phase of the World Cup. Four minutes later, however, Johnny Rep scored for them and it was all over.

'So I was lucky that I scored a good goal in the World Cup with billions watching. It could have happened on a Saturday at the Baseball Ground against Ipswich or Reading and no one would have known about it, but that's life.'

Archie pauses for a moment, glancing around Pride Park Stadium. 'This place is brilliant,' he says, 'and I will always be grateful for the opportunity to play under two top-class managers at Derby County and to play for the fans too. Derby supporters always turned up in their droves, even when times were bad.'

1984–85 **Bobby Davison**

It spoke volumes for the wholehearted style of Bobby Davison that when the final whistle sounded he inevitably dragged himself from the Baseball Ground wearing a shirt caked in mud. The never-say-die striker who became the new hero of Rams fans throughout an often tempestuous period in the 1980s arrived in Derby a year after the legendary Kevin Hector had scored his 200th goal in his second spell with the club.

Davison and Hector never played together for the Rams, and the two prolific goalscorers were miles apart in the way they approached the game. While Hector had an incredible balance that appeared to allow him to skim the surface of the Baseball Ground bog as defenders sank in his wake, Davison loved to throw himself about in the mud and dive in among opponents' boots.

In their best years both had searing pace, but it is a tribute to Davison's goalscoring instinct that the 26 goals he recorded in the 1985–86 Division Three promotion season was not only better than anything Hector ever achieved in a single campaign; it was the best return since Ray Straw's 37 in 1956–57.

Bobby Davison.

'Bobby, Bobby, Bobby, Bobby Davison' the crowd chanted as the ball kept hitting the back of the net, and for five consecutive seasons from 1982–83 until he departed for Leeds United for £350,000 in November 1987 the popular striker was the club's top scorer in every campaign. The spearhead of two promotions in successive years for Arthur Cox's resurgent Rams, he was given a hero's welcome when he returned on loan to bang in eight goals in just 10 games in 1992 to give Derby a much-needed lift after relegation.

Born in South Shields, Davison was a late starter in League football, signing for Huddersfield Town at the age of 21. After only two appearances in a year, Bobby moved on to Halifax Town in the summer of 1981 and was scoring at an average of a goal every other game by the time Derby were drawn against Halifax in the first round of the Milk Cup at the start of the 1982–83 season. Davison was on the score sheet as the Fourth

Bobby celebrates as another goal goes in.

Division outfit pulled off a shock 2–1 victory in the first leg at The Shay, and he scored twice at the Baseball Ground in the return leg as the Rams struggled through 5–2 after extra-time.

Davison's potential, painfully obvious to the Derby central-defenders (George Foster and John McAlle) who tried to mark him over the two legs, was apparently missed by manager John Newman, whose dreadful side managed only one victory in the first 16 League fixtures. It was left to new manager Peter Taylor, who replaced Newman in the November, to snap up Davison's services for a mere £80,000. The recommendation actually came from Roy McFarland, newly installed as Taylor's assistant, who had targeted the prolific striker the previous season while managing Bradford City.

Taylor, who was given the credit for being Brian Clough's talent-spotter-in-chief during the pair's most successful managerial years, did not pull off many spectacular captures during a pretty dismal second spell with the Rams, but the signing of Davison was a gem. While other acquisitions, the likes of Paul Hooks, Calvin Plummer, Bobby Campbell and former Forest heroes Kenny Burns and John Robertson, only succeeded in hastening Derby's spectacular slide into the Third Division, Bobby flourished.

The new signing was given his first taste of Second Division football as a 73rd-minute substitute, as Taylor and McFarland's side recorded Derby's first League win in three months against Rotherham United at the Baseball Ground on 4 December 1982. Replacing John Richards in attack, Bobby set about his task with customary enthusiasm, and the Rams won 3–0 thanks to two goals from David Swindlehurst and one from Ian Dalziel. A substitute again in the next two games, a defeat at Fulham and a home draw against Crystal Palace, Bobby's full debut came two days after Christmas in a single-goal defeat at Newcastle's St James' Park.

Still no goals, but before the year was out Bobby had bagged his first brace for his new club in a bizarre home match against Shrewsbury Town. The Rams went 3–0 down before a late flurry from Davison gave the home crowd something to cheer about as he registered two typically spectacular goals. First he placed a flashing header from Mick Brolly's centre past Shrewsbury 'keeper Steve Ogrizovic, and minutes later fired home again from a seemingly impossible angle.

Bobby was off the mark and, by the end of a campaign that had at one time threatened relegation but ended in a relatively respectable 13th-place finish, he and Swindlehurst were joint leading scorers in the League with eight goals apiece.

He was an instant hit with the fans, and not only because of his goalscoring prowess. He was a worker, always willing to track back, harass opponents when they had the ball and kick-start another Derby attack. Bobby was no goal-hanger, the type of explosive striker who conserved his energy for when the big chance came, he was an all-action hero. Even when denied service from his own players, Bobby would chase every opportunity to create something for the team.

The season that followed, 1983–84, was a disaster for the club with relegation and near extinction following a winding-up order in the High Court, but Bobby managed to score 17 times, including an FA Cup fourth-round hat-trick against non-League Telford United. Manager Taylor quit in April 1984, leaving McFarland in charge for the remaining nine League games. Even a Davison double in a win over Portsmouth in the last home game of the campaign was not enough as the Rams fell five points short of safety and headed for Division Three for the first time since 1957.

Bobby was unquestionably the star of the club's centenary season. After guiding Newcastle United back to the top flight, Arthur Cox had fallen out with the Magpies over contractual issues and arrived

Bobby waits for a chance to pounce.

as Derby's ninth manager in 11 years, McFarland staying on as his assistant. Davison played every game in 1984–85 (53 in total) scoring 26 goals. Early on he played second fiddle to strike partner Kevin Wilson, who started the season in scintillating form with 13 goals in the opening 11 games. But in the 13th minute of the home game against Plymouth on 13 October Wilson broke his arm and spent eight weeks on the sidelines, playing only three more times on his return before being transferred to Ipswich Town for £150,000.

Cox used the cash wisely, buying Trevor Christie to partner Davison up front and also adding to the quality of his midfield in the shape of Geraint Williams and Gary Micklewhite.

Unbeaten in their final five games, the Rams finished seventh and Bobby was Player of the Season. The club was now owned by Robert Maxwell, and the future looked more assured.

Davison was top scorer again with 23 goals in all competitions as Derby clinched promotion from Division Three with a home win in the penultimate game against Rotherham United and, now partnered by Phil Gee, he proved he was also much too good for Division Two defences, hitting 22 goals as Cox's side ran away with the title to record successive

Bobby has just scored and Nigel Callaghan goes to congratulate him in the Rams' 2–1 win over Leeds United at the Baseball Ground in May 1987 which ensured promotion to the top flight. They went from the Third Division to the First in two seasons.

Bobby Davison heads goalwards in the Rams' 1–0 win over Ipswich Town at the Baseball Ground in November 1991.

All-action hero Davison is floored as he breaks away at the Baseball Ground.

promotions. Gee, signed from local side Gresley Rovers, chipped in with 17 goals in a side now marshalled by ex-England midfielder John Gregory. Typically, it was a Davison goal in a 2–1 Baseball Ground victory over Leeds United on 2 May 1987 that clinched promotion. Restored to the side following treatment for a knee ligament injury, Bobby forced his way through a cluster of defenders to head Micklewhite's centre past goalkeeper Mervyn Day to add to Gee's earlier strike.

Amid the excitement of signing England internationals Peter Shilton and Mark Wright to bolster Cox's squad for the top flight, it still left many fans perplexed when Davison was allowed to go to Leeds United in November 1987 after scoring once in 13 First Division League games. Although youth product Andy Garner was a willing replacement, Gee struggled without his regular partner, and the signing of veteran striker Frank Stapleton on loan the following March was not a success.

Bobby proved he was not a one-hit wonder, and he was soon a cult hero at Leeds as Howard Wilkinson galvanised the West Yorkshire club into a side good enough not only for promotion to Division One but into one that would become top-flight champions as well. Davison clicked with the Elland Road crowd in the same way he had with the fans at the Baseball Ground. A hard-working goalscorer is universally admired, and Bobby was still good enough in his early 30s to score 35 goals in 110 games for Leeds.

The striker must curse his luck that he missed the Rams' Division One exploits as Dean Saunders grabbed the goals and the plaudits, and he returned only after the excitement had subsided and Derby County – now owned by local businessman Lionel Pickering – were back in Division Two. Brought back from Leeds on loan in September 1991, Bobby staged an engaging cameo that started with a

Goal! Bobby celebrates with the Popside.

goalscoring comeback win over Brighton at the Baseball Ground to break a win-less streak for Cox's side. It was truly a hero's return. His presence in the team that day put 2,000 on the attendance, and when Davison ran onto Paul Williams's pass two minutes before half-time to score his 99th Derby goal it was business as usual. An initial month-long loan was extended, and Bobby scored eight times in 10 games, his final strike a last-minute opportunist goal that was the winner in a tense 3–2 victory at Bristol Rovers on 23 November.

Davison's new strike partner Ian Ormondroyd signed on loan from Aston Villa in the same week Bobby arrived from Leeds and was offered a permanent contract in December 1991. Bobby was not, and he returned to Leeds before going out on loan again that season to Sheffield United. Ironically, Ormondroyd's Derby career was to be short. He scored eight goals in 25 League games before being used as a makeweight with Phil Gee in the £1.3 million record signing of Leicester City's Paul Kitson in March 1992.

Davison was close to promotion success with two Second Division sides – Leicester City and Sheffield United – and played also for Rotherham United and Hull City before his retirement during the 1995–96 season.

A manager at non-League Guiseley for a short period in 2000, he coached at Bradford City and Sheffield United before in 2008 becoming an advisory coach, then head coach, at Hungarian side Ferencváros.

It is no surprise that many fans who grew up with the Derby County of the early 1980s, rate Bobby Davison, who is 10th in the club's all-time goalscoring charts, as their all-time favourite player.

1985–86 **Ross MacLaren**

Never was a man more thankful that he had missed two penalties during Derby County's Third Division promotion campaign of 1985–86. With the end in sight, the Rams, having played marvellous football for most the season, were experiencing a serious attack of the jitters and desperately needed a win from their penultimate game – at the Baseball Ground against Rotherham United – to guarantee promotion alongside champions Reading and second-placed Plymouth Argyle. With just seven minutes remaining and the scores level at 1–1, the referee pointed to the spot, and it was Trevor Christie, rather than the newly crowned Player of the Year Ross MacLaren, who stepped up to take the most nerve-jarring of spot-kicks.

MacLaren, in his first season at the Baseball Ground after signing in the summer of 1985 from Shrewsbury Town, had started the campaign as the designated penalty taker and had tucked one away in a 2–0 win at Cardiff City at the end of September. Then he missed one in the emphatic 5–1 home pasting of Swansea City, but it mattered not. Jeff Chandler assumed responsibility for penalty duties,

Manager Arthur Cox presents Ross MacLaren with the Player of the Year award in May 1986.

Ross MacLaren celebrates on a rainy night in May 1986 when the Rams beat Rotherham United 2–1 at the Baseball Ground to seal promotion to Division Two.

scoring one in the next match, a Baseball Ground victory over Notts County, but as the season reached its climax MacLaren was the man again, scoring from the spot in a 1–1 home draw against lowly Bury on the last day of April, but also missing one in the same game.

With points desperately needed, it was a crucial miss and when the biggest decision of the campaign was made by referee Mr Fitzharris of Bolton in the 83rd minutes against Rotherham, MacLaren was a relieved man indeed as Christie, who had warmed up with a successful spot-kick three days earlier in a 3–0 win at Swansea, placed the ball on the penalty spot in front of a crowd of just over 21,000 nervous souls at the Baseball Ground – easily the highest home League attendance of the season.

Only six minutes earlier Arthur Cox's team seemed to have the points wrapped up when MacLaren hit a superb clearance out of defence, Christie dummied and the 21-year-old Phil Gee, signed from non-League Gresley Rovers the previous summer and on as a substitute for the injured George Williams, ran in on goal to gleefully slot past the Rotherham 'keeper for the first of his 31 goals for the Rams. 'Two minutes later Mark Wallington came for a cross and dropped it at their striker's feet and we started getting a bit edgy,' Ross tells me. 'Luckily enough we got a free-kick on the edge of their box, which I took, and one of their lads was adjudged to have elbowed Jeff Chandler in the box, which I thought at the time was a bit dubious. But we got the penalty, and I was absolutely delighted it was Trevor taking it and not me! What a wonderful day it was!'

Born in Edinburgh, Ross had been a trainee at Rangers before moving south of the border with Shrewsbury. He was 23 years old when Arthur Cox snapped him up from Shrewsbury in the summer of 1985. Other summer captures included Chandler and Steve McClaren, but the new ambition of the Maxwell-owned club was seriously signalled in November of 1985 when John Gregory, an England international 18 months previously, agreed to step down to the Third Division in a £100,000 transfer from Queen's Park Rangers.

'Once I drove down to the Baseball Ground and saw the size of the stadium and the enthusiasm of the spectators I always knew we would win things, especially after a good pre-season,' says Ross, who in addition to being a tidy defender was also a great passer and striker of a ball.

It was a gruelling campaign of 60 matches, including two in the Freight Rover Trophy, and new signing MacLaren was an ever present in the League, FA and League Cups. Third place in those days meant automatic promotion as the Play-off system (that would often dog Derby's progress in the future – but also on one glorious occasion bring success) had yet to be introduced. 'It was a fantastic feeling to come to a new club and be Player of the Year in my first season,' says Ross. 'I always felt I had a rapport with the fans, and it was an honour to receive the award.'

One of the reasons MacLaren settled in so quickly was the partnership he forged in central-defence with inspirational captain Rob Hindmarch, the man-mountain snapped up on a free transfer from Sunderland by the canny Cox in July 1984. Hindmarch, who went on to play 196 games for the Rams before a £300,000 transfer to Wolves in the summer of 1990, died from motor neurone disease, aged only 41. 'Rob was a great lad and a fantastic captain,' says Ross. 'He was a joy to play with. I knew exactly what he was doing. He would always attack things and would expect me to sweep up behind him, and that's why we created a good partnership.'

MacLaren was an ever present again in 1986–87 and admitted few people expected the same squad to run away with the Second Division title. But Bobby Davison and Phil Gee were unstoppable as a new twin strike-force, scoring 34 goals between them in the League as Cox's side recorded a six-point advantage over second-placed Portsmouth. 'Davo was already a legend when I arrived at Derby, and he just carried it on, but I think we were all surprised how well we did that season. We hadn't expected that Phil Gee would come into the side and score a lot of goals, but we took it by storm and won a

John Gregory (right) and Ross MacLaren line up for Derby in 1986. MacLaren later worked under Gregory when the former Rams player was manager of Villa and then at Pride Park.

Eric Steele runs out as Ross MacLaren bars Ian Baird's way in the Rams' 2–1 win over Leeds United at the Baseball Ground in May 1987 which ensured promotion to the top flight.

record number of away matches. I think teams under-estimated us.

'The so-called football experts thought we would be a mid-table side, but we believed in ourselves and went into every match with the mindset that we wouldn't get beaten, and most of the time that's what happened.'

Only Gary Micklewhite and MacLaren started every League game during successive promotions, and Ross tells me: 'It was a great achievement to stay clear of injury and not to be dropped by the manager for two seasons. It was hard work as well, but always enjoyable.'

Now came an even bigger challenge as a squad bolstered by the arrival of England internationals Peter Shilton and Mark Wright prepared to test themselves in Division One, and MacLaren realised he was no longer guaranteed to be one of the first names on Cox's team sheet. 'Playing in the top division, Arthur Cox was always going to want to bring in new players to strengthen his squad and, with Mark Wright being an international, that was a great challenge for me and for Rob. He was top quality, and we had Shilts as well. Changes were inevitable, and before long Paul Blades came into the centre and I moved to full-back.'

MacLaren started 25 League games in the top flight and was a substitute nine times, signing off at right-back in the 0–0 draw against Everton at the Baseball Ground on 2 May 1988. The defender, who had played in three different divisions in three exciting seasons for a resurgent Derby, was transferred to Swindon Town in the summer of 1988 for £165,000. Five years later he was their captain in the Premiership. 'I think you know when your time is up,' he says. 'I had three great years with two

Rob Hindmarch (right) and Ross MacLaren pictured in February 1987.

promotions, and we retained our place in the First Division. I really enjoyed it and the people, and the club were really good to me, but things come to an end.'

On retirement Ross became Swindon's reserve-team coach before linking up again with John Gregory as chief scout at Aston Villa. He was back at Derby County as coach when Gregory was appointed manager at Pride Park in February 2002. A little over a year later both departed, and Ross worked for Southend and Notts County before settling back in Derbyshire to run the Blue Bell at Kirk Langley. 'It's a lovely place to live. Especially when I go back to Pride Park, I get such a big welcome and still get asked for autographs, and that's a fantastic feeling,' he says. 'I miss the day-to-day involvement of football, the training and being with the boys, but I have a business to run and you move on, just like you do as a footballer, and hope for better things. It's hard work, but I'm enjoying it.'

1986–87 **Geraint Williams**

George Williams recalls turning to a member of the Bristol Rovers coaching staff on the team bus in Derby and commenting enthusiastically: 'What a fantastic place to play football!' The chap on the receiving end of the Welshman's fervour could be forgiven a raised eyebrow after a scoreless Division Three scrap fought on the Baseball Ground's infamous cloying March mud. So far as George was concerned however, his introduction to the home of the Rams in 1985 was a case of love at first sight. Just a couple of days later it became a match made in heaven when Derby County's manager Arthur Cox made a bid for the diminutive Rovers player who had terrorised his central-midfielders that March afternoon. 'The Baseball Ground was a proper football stadium,' George tells me. 'The atmosphere that day, even with a crowd of only 10,000, was fantastic.

'That said, it didn't even cross my mind I might move to Derby. In any case I was getting married that summer and I was settled at Bristol. Then on the Tuesday after the Baseball Ground match I was called into the manager David Williams's office and told Rovers had received an offer from Derby and accepted it. I drove up that night to meet Arthur Cox. There was a reserve game on, and even for that the atmosphere was special. I chatted to Arthur and made my mind up very quickly.'

Cox paid £43,500 on the eve of the transfer deadline to make George a Derby player. It was money well spent for a combative midfielder who went on to play 332 games for the Rams in three divisions over the next seven years.

In 1985 Derby County were re-emerging from the dark days, albeit slowly. Consigned to the third tier of English football amid winding up petitions in the High Court and an unlikely

managerial comeback by Peter Taylor, the Rams were no great shakes in the Third Division, even under the stewardship of Cox, the club's ninth manager in 11 years.

Season 1984–85 would see a club that just a decade before had been England's finest claim seventh place in Division Three behind champions Bradford City, Millwall, Hull City, Gillingham and both Bristol clubs. However, as George Williams strode out to make his debut at Brentford's inhospitable Griffin Park on 30 March 1985 – an event witnessed by 4,423 fans – he was getting aboard a Rams roller coaster that, for once in the club's turbulent history, promised more thrills than spills.

Gary Micklewhite scored Derby's goal that day as they drew 1–1 with Brentford. Cox's line up was: Sutton, Streete, Buckley, Lewis, Hindmarch, Blades, Micklewhite, Christie, Davison, Williams and Robertson.

In the front car of the roller coaster was Cox. Like so many others who played for the Rams during the Cox years, George is fiercely loyal in his support of his former boss.

Geraint Williams with his memento of being voted the Player of the Year.

Geraint Williams (left), Phil Gee and Nigel Callaghan on a lap of honour after the Rams' 2–1 win over Leeds United to ensure promotion to the top flight.

'Arthur was the kind of guy you would happily go through a brick wall for – but you also knew he would probably get there first and be smashing down the bricks by the time you arrived,' says George. 'Arthur was a leader of men, and in those days especially it was like we were all going into war together. He engendered an incredible team spirit, to the extent that after games we would all go into town together, 10 or 12 players and partners.'

Ask George to name his favourite teammate from his Derby days and he chooses another warrior – Rob Hindmarch, the former Rams captain whose life was tragically cut short by motor neurone disease. 'Rob was the type of person you would want to go to war with,' says George. 'He was there at the start. What a character and what a leader.'

All this talk of wars, battles and leaders is verging on overkill (if you'll excuse the turn of phrase), but it sums up the spirit and passion that George brought to the club. He was that type of player. Which makes the revelation of how a young Geraint Williams actually got landed with the nickname 'George' all the more surprising. 'This is a bit of an exclusive for you,' he says 'but when I was a little lad in the Valleys I always had a ball at my feet, and the locals would say "Just look at him dribbling…like a little Georgie Best!" So in time the name "George" stuck. Anyone who played with me or against me would be amused to discover I was once considered to be Wales's answer to George Best, but that's the way it happened! I'm still "George" to this day, or "Gaffer" of course to the players at Colchester. Only members of my family call me "Geraint".'

In his first full season, 1985–86, the Rams won promotion to the old Second Division, and as George happily conquered the muddy wastelands of the Baseball Ground he played alongside a couple of cultured midfielders who might also have fancied themselves as George Bests in their early years. 'Steve McClaren was a very good footballer, an elegant player,' says George. 'Then he got injured, John Gregory came along and Steve found it difficult to get back. Both were intelligent players, but I can't claim to have predicted Steve would one day go on to manage England – it wasn't that obvious. Credit to him, though, he had to finish early through injury, and he made himself into an excellent coach.'

Injury was something George miraculously steered clear of during his time with the Rams, and his name always seemed to be on the team sheet. I ask if this was luck or simply a willingness at times to play through the pain barrier. 'A bit of both, I suppose,' he replies. 'You always have to be sensible with injuries because some you just make worse by playing on. But if it was something like a broken nose or a knock, Arthur would say to me "You are okay to play, aren't you George?" And I would say, "Of course!".'

Successive promotions meant Derby were back in the top flight in 1987, and George, who had joined

George pictured managing Colchester United against Derby County.

Geraint Williams (left), physiotheraptist Gordon Guthrie and Rob Hindmarch celebrate the winning of the old Second Division Championship after Derby County beat Plymouth Argyle 4–2 at the Baseball Ground in May 1987.

the club two tiers down, was determined to prove himself against the likes of Liverpool and Manchester United, especially after Derby's fans made him their Player of the Year as the Rams romped away with the Second Division title. 'A lot of good players left the club along the way, but I wanted to be part of everything as we progressed,' he says. 'I could see the club was going places, and to keep up I worked harder than ever. One of my favourite games in a Derby shirt was beating Leeds at the Baseball Ground. We needed to draw that game to be sure of promotion, and we played brilliantly and beat them 2–1.'

Another notable game from season 1986–87 was a victory at Stoke in November when a goal from George – a rare feat, but always worth the wait – contributed to a 2–0 victory. 'I bent one into the top corner that day, and no one could believe it,' he laughs. 'We were under incredible pressure from Stoke. At one stage there was a big pile-up on our line – almost like a rugby scrum with about 15 players involved and the ball bouncing around all over the place. Finally it somehow ended up in Mark Wallington's hands, and Arthur said to us afterwards, "After surviving that I reckon you lot have a chance of going up this year!".'

George relished the top-flight years, especially the second season in the old First Division when Derby finished fifth and were the only side to do the double over eventual champions Arsenal. The dependable

Geraint Williams pictured in April 1992.

midfielder missed only one game in Derby's first three Division One seasons, during which time a 6–0 home thrashing of Manchester City in 1989–90 soon became a favourite.

The Rams were relegated the following season as financial pressures re-emerged during the chairmanship of Robert Maxwell. George was made captain of a side that fought back well with third place in Division Two in 1991–92. 'It was a huge honour being made captain when you look at the tradition of the club and the men who have led the side down the years,' he recalls. 'I had seven fantastic years at Derby, and I'm sad we fell away at the end.'

While Cox's Derby narrowly missed out on promotion in 1992, George was quickly back in the top flight when Ipswich Town paid £650,000 for his services. Typically, he was also influential at Portman Road, and by the time he hung up his boots as a player at Colchester he had chalked up 650 League appearances.

After seven years as coach and assistant manager at Layer Road, George was thrust into the hot seat at Colchester, and I caught up with him after a scouting mission to Pride Park Stadium. 'The Derby public are always very welcoming,' he said. 'The fans outside the main entrance with their autograph books are the same guys who used to wait outside the players' entrance at the Baseball Ground, Marian McMinn was still on the front desk and Gordon Guthrie was still on the bench, looking younger than he did in my day! There's still a family feel to the club.

'Football always meant so much to the people of Derby, and I for one felt the responsibility on my shoulders. When you put on the shirt, it really did mean something.

'When I went away on international duty with Wales, my teammates used to say "It must be horrible to have to play at the Baseball Ground", but I put them right. I told them Derby was only a horrible place to play if you were the opposition!'

1987–88 **Michael Forsyth**

Of the four debutants that took the field at Oldham Athletic's Boundary Park for the first game of the 1986–87 season, Michael Forsyth was destined to make the most of his Derby County career. A typically canny Arthur Cox signing the previous March, Forsyth did not feature at all in the side that won promotion from the Third Division in 1985–86. Steve Buckley had been a fixture at full-back for the previous eight years and, while Bucko saw out an impressive 366-game career, Forsyth played in central-defence, his recognised position, for the reserves as Derby became the first Third Division club to win the Central League.

Not only was Buckley a legend, he was a relic from the First Division days of the 1970s, and it would take some player to get anywhere near his appearance record. Forsyth beat it with 403 starts in the next eight years – and he *was* some player.

The other three who made their debuts in a disappointing opening day defeat at Oldham in August 1987 were Forsyth's full-back partner in the coming years Mel Sage, striker Mark Lillis, who scored one goal in only eight starts for the Rams, and the unfortunate Steve Cross, whose promising Derby career was spoiled by injuries.

Forsyth had played only 29 times in three seasons for West Bromwich Albion, the club he joined as

Michael Forsyth.

an apprentice. Signing as a professional in 1983, 'Bruce', as he was known to teammates for obvious reasons, made his debut aged only 17 against Arsenal at Highbury, marking Tony Woodcock and Charlie Nicholas. West Brom won 1–0, and the following week for his home debut he was up against Ian Rush and Kenny Dalglish as Liverpool won by the odd goal in three at the Hawthorns. Just ahead of the transfer deadline in March 1986, Ron Saunders – in the job only a matter of weeks after taking over from Nobby Stiles as the Baggies' manager – decided he'd seen enough of Forsyth and was in the process of loaning the defender out to Northampton Town when Cox stepped in, paying £22,500 for his services. It was a steal. Nine years and more than 400 games later, Derby banked a huge profit by selling the defender to Notts County for £200,000.

Already an England Youth international, he was good enough during his Derby career to represent his country at Under-21 level, making his debut against Switzerland in Lausanne in May 1988, and later was an England B international.

Michael Forsyth hooks in a spectacular shot watched by Andy Comyn and Paul Simpson in the goalless draw with Cambridge United at the Baseball Ground in April 1992.

Though not as threatening going forward as the man he replaced in the number-three shirt, Forsyth was taller, which made him more useful under the high ball, and his no-nonsense tackling was often ferocious. His gradual improvement throughout that first season with Derby was mirrored by the team, which made an average start but went on to win the Second Division title with six points to spare over second-placed Portsmouth.

A confidence booster for Forsyth and the team came against Sunderland at the Baseball Ground, a night match on 1 October 1986, on the back of a disappointing home draw against Millwall and defeat at Bruce's former club West Brom.

There was an air of despondency about the old ground when the Black Cats went two up, then both John Gregory and George Williams took control of the centre of the park, and when the ball came back to Forsyth from a Gary Micklewhite corner he fired home a low shot from the edge of the penalty area for his first Derby goal. The recovery was underway, Forsyth suddenly looked a more impressive player altogether and the Rams equalised through Bobby Davison after good work from Phil Gee. Sage hit the winner – also his first goal for the club – and Cox's side went through the entire campaign unbeaten on home soil.

Despite the high-profile signings of England internationals Peter Shilton and Mark Wright in the summer of 1987, Foysyth made the Rams' first season back in the First Division his year. In an echo of the successful early Clough years, manager Cox was able to field his first choice side consistently throughout the campaign, and three players – Shilton, Williams and winger Nigel Callaghan – did not miss a League game all season. Forsyth missed only one, as did Gregory, and it was the reliable left-back rather than the more fêted names, who took the fans' vote as Player of the Year as Derby finished a creditable 15th. For good measure, Bruce contributed three goals that season, two of which came in consecutive League matches.

He was on target in a 2–2 home draw against Sheffield Wednesday on 19 September, but his most celebrated goal was the equaliser in the 1–1 thriller at the Baseball Ground against Liverpool. It came five minutes from the end of a night game in March 1988 against the eventual champions. Forsyth started it and finished it, first rampaging into attack before finding Micklewhite, on as a substitute for recent signing Ted McMinn. When the winger's low centre came in, Forsyth, who had not stopped running, was perfectly placed to fire home, sending the home crowd delirious with delight.

After recording eight consecutive League defeats between December and February, Cox's team were bouncing back, and for good measure Forsyth was on the score sheet again three days later in a 3–0 victory at Coventry City. Though not yet mathematically safe going into the final game of the campaign against Everton, Derby eventually finished eight points clear of relegation, and Cox had a launch-pad for 1988–89, which was to be the Rams' most impressive season in recent memory.

Dean Saunders arrived to score the goals, and Derby finished fifth behind champions Arsenal, Liverpool, Forest and Norwich City. Forsyth was one of three players who did not miss a League game all season (the other two were Shilton and Paul Blades), and the full-back was an ever present again in 1989–90.

Though Cox's side were back in the Second Division by 1991, Bruce was still a regular and took part

'Bruce' pictured after signing on for Burton Albion.

in two unsuccessful Play-off campaigns, including the Final against Leicester City in 1994. His last game for Derby was as a substitute for his successor in the number-three shirt, Shane Nicholson, in a 3–2 home defeat against Sheffield United on 4 February 1995.

He could not prevent his new club Notts County being relegated that season and stayed at Meadow Lane only until December 1996 when former teammate John Gregory invited him to play for Wycombe Wanderers. A serious leg injury in March 1998 kept Bruce out of the side for more than 12 months, and although he returned towards the end of the 1998–99 campaign injury eventually forced him out of League football. After gaining his coaching badges (he was on the Derby County Academy staff for a short time) he returned to Wycombe as a part-time coach during the 2000–2001 season, taking over as reserve-team manager in the summer of 2001.

In between times he was invited by Burton Albion manager Nigel Clough to resume his playing career at non-League level. 'Nigel called me and wanted to know if I'd be interested in

Trophy winner Forsyth in his Derby days.

helping them out against Woking as they'd got through to the FA Cup first round,' Bruce says. 'I hadn't kicked a ball for six months and I hadn't done any work with a ball at all, but I said yes and ended up playing there for a season and a half. I had a really good time. Clough is brilliant, and I really learnt a lot off him as well.'

A career in football management seemed inevitable, and on his full-time appointment at Wycombe Forsyth announced: 'I was a pro for 16 years, which was brilliant, and luckily enough I'm still involved in the game, and hopefully I can pass on some of my knowledge to others.'

Not long afterwards, he accelerated away from football into the fast lane of motor racing, joining Jenson Button's F1 back-up team.

1988–89 & 1989–90 **Mark Wright**

Oooo Mark Wright! The familiar cry from the Baseball Ground terraces might very well initially have been one of astonishment as the Rams, back in the top flight after an absence of seven years, smashed their transfer record to sign an established England centre-half from Southampton for £760,000 in August 1987. Beating the £410,000 paid seven years earlier for David Swindlehurst, the capture of Wright came only weeks after Derby manager Arthur Cox had already raided The Dell to bring in England's number one Peter Shilton.

Barely three years after being the subject of a winding-up petition in the High Court issued by the Inland Revenue and Customs and Excise, Derby County were back in business. Cox had achieved successive promotions from the Third Division and, with the backing of chairman Robert Maxwell's apparently limitless financial resources, these were exciting times for the Rams' supporters.

Wright in action at the Baseball Ground.

Aside from the acquisitions of Wright and Shilton, Cox was seemingly content to stick with the squad that had lifted the Second Division title in 1987 with a six-point cushion over second-placed Portsmouth. Shilton took over from Mark Wallington in goal (ironically, Wallington had been Shilton's replacement at Leicester City 13 years earlier when the country's best 'keeper made his first high-profile move to Stoke City) and Wright, not signed in time to feature in the an opening-game home win over Luton Town or a draw at Queen's Park Rangers four days later, slipped in as captain and centre-half alongside a choice of either of the promotion-winning side's centre-backs Rob Hindmarch and Ross MacLaren, or sometimes Paul Blades.

Wright's debut at the Baseball Ground came on 29 August against Wimbledon, the power-house team of the top flight, whose aerial barrage troubled even the best players at that time. John Fashanu's goal brought to an end Derby's year-long unbeaten home sequence, but neither Wright nor Shilton missed a game for the remainder of the season, and it was largely due to their influence and presence that Cox's side kept their heads above water, finishing 15th ahead of West Ham, Charlton, Chelsea and the three

Mark Wright clears the ball in the goalless draw against Portsmouth at the Baseball Ground in September 1987.

relegated clubs, Portsmouth, Watford and Oxford United, as Liverpool strolled to the title.

Not since the days of McFarland and Todd had the Derby crowd seen a centre-back of the stature of Wright. Tall, powerful, fast and composed on the ball, he had everything. Including, at times, a quick temper. He fell out with England manager Bobby Robson after a disastrous 1988 European Championships. Both Wright and Shilton played in the opening group match against the Republic of Ireland, which Jack Charlton's Irish won 1–0, and then in the next match, a defeat in Shilton's 100th international by Holland, for whom Marco Van Basten scored a hat-trick.

Robson had given Wright his international debut as a 20-year-old against Wales in May 1984, only four years after the centre-half signed professional forms at Oxford United. It took only 11 senior appearances to attract the attention of Southampton, who snapped up both Wright and Keith Cassells in a March 1982 deal that took a future Derby player, Trevor Hebberd, to Oxford, plus £80,000. Kevin Keegan was in the Saints side when Wright, still only 18, made his debut in the First Division the following month. In his first full season he was Southampton's Player of the Year, and after winning international recognition it was a shock to fans when Lawrie McMenemy accepted Derby's approach, although without Wright and Shilton, the south-coast club still managed to finish three places above the Rams in 1987–88.

Wright was in imperious form the following season – the first of two consecutive Player of the Year campaigns for the defender. Derby County's fifth-place finish in 1988–89 would not be bettered in the succeeding 20 years, and Wright was at his very best as the Rams missed out on European qualification only because of the ban on English clubs following the 1985 Heysel disaster.

What is easily forgotten, however, is that the campaign started badly. In the first seven weeks of the season only two players managed to get the ball in the net: Hebberd, signed that summer from Oxford

United, and Paul Goddard, another August signing and a somewhat belated replacement for Bobby Davison, who had joined Leeds United for £350,000 the previous November. The search for a regular goalscorer was made all the more urgent by Phil Gee's ankle injury sustained in a fiesty 1–1 September draw at Forest's City Ground, and the early season rumour was that the much-travelled Lee Chapman might be on his way to the Baseball Ground.

The home defeat to Norwich City on 8 October 1988, was a bad day for the Rams. They failed to score for the third successive game and though the result left them in 12th place, they were only a point clear of the relegation zone. Worse still, Wright failed to complete the game after being sent off in the 55th minute. The red mist decended when the Canaries' Trevor Putney started to kick lumps out of crowd favourite Ted McMinn. Despite being floored by a tackle, the 'Tin Man' managed to trap the ball between his legs to the irritation of Putney, who started to stamp on the winger. Wright raced 25 yards to grab Putney by the throat, and although Cox jumped from the dug-out to pull his captain away the damage had been done and both Wright and Putney were shown red cards by referee Alan Seville. It was the first of three sendings-off during Wright's Derby career and was prompted undoubtedly by his loyalty and friendship towards McMinn, who later became his assistant during early managerial jobs.

In the time it took Wright to sit out a two-game suspension Dean Saunders had become Derby's first £1 million signing, and the former Oxford striker set about his work with relish, scoring two on debut in the 4–1 home defeat of Wimbledon. Wright was back for the 3–1 victory at White Hart Lane on 5 November when Saunders scored again and McMinn hit two. In Shilton, Wright and Saunders, the Rams had three world-class performers and were a match for anyone, including champions Arsenal, whom they beat at Highbury in the penultimate game of the season thanks to another brace from Saunders.

The lack of investment from Maxwell after such a successful campaign puzzled Rams fans, and the only way was down in 1989–

Wright climbs all over an opponent in the Rams' 2–0 defeat by Luton Town at Kenilworth Road on the last day of the 1990–91 season.

Mark Wright is appointed the new Oxford United manager, with his assistant Ted McMinn, in May 2001.

90. Both Wright and Shilton were still important to England and Saunders managed 18 goals as an ever present, but the campaign was an anti-climax. Cox's side finished only three points clear of the relegation zone in 16th place, and Wright was again the best player, scoring six goals in 36 League starts, including one in the 6–0 demolition of Manchester City at the Baseball Ground in November 1989. It proved to be the highlight of the season.

A troubling domestic campaign lay in store, but first Wright had time to emerge as one of the stars of the 1990 World Cup in Italy. Impressive as a sweeper in a side that reached the semi-finals before losing out on penalties to eventual winners Germany, Wright scored his only England goal during the tournament and it was a vital one – a header from Paul Gascoigne's free-kick against Egypt ensuring that Bobby Robson's side progressed beyond the group stage.

Wright's displays for England that summer made him a target for top clubs, and by the time he captained England against the USSR in May 1991 Derby were already relegated and a £2.3 million move to Liverpool was only a matter of months away.

Chairman Maxwell, an absentee landlord unloved by Rams supporters, put the club in a state of limbo when he announced Derby County was for sale, and it meant that throughout the 1990–91 season manager Cox was unable to sign a player or even bring one in on loan. Relegation was inevitable despite the presence of Shilton, Wright and Saunders, who signed off with 17 League goals before joining Liverpool for £2.9 million just four days after Wright. The incoming cash was used to pay off Maxwell.

As captain of the Anfield club, Wright led Liverpool to an FA Cup Final victory the following season, but his time there was beset by injuries. Four years after his previous international call-up, Terry Venables recalled him to the England side for a friendly against Croatia in April 1996 and he won the last of his 45 caps the following month against Hungary.

Mark Wright retired as a player in 1998 and became manager of Conference side Southport the following year before moving into League management with the club at which he started his football career, Oxford United. He later managed Chester City and Peterborough United and was also keen at one stage for Jim Smith to take him onto the coaching staff at Derby County.

1990–91 **Dean Saunders**

It says something of the quality of a footballer when he is able to play the glorious game with a smile on his face. Dean Saunders was one of a happy band of great footballers who thoroughly enjoyed his time on the pitch. And when he was smiling, it invariably meant he had notched another goal.

'Deano' thrilled the Baseball Ground crowds for three top-flight seasons from 1988 to 1991 after becoming the Rams' first £1 million signing. Incredibly, he missed only one match during his time at the club – a League Cup fixture for which he was ineligible. When he signed for Liverpool for almost £3 million – a British domestic record – he had chalked up 130 consecutive appearances.

'I loved playing football, and I still do, even today,' he tells me. 'I was coaching some kids recently, and without even realising what I was doing I ended up joining in their game and trying my best to score a goal! One of the other coaches commented afterwards how desperate I was to score. I didn't consciously play with smile on my face, but my biggest strength was my enthusiasm for football, and that's why I smiled.'

As for the ever-present record at Derby, Dean explains: 'Not many people know that I did my cruciate ligament when I was 17, and that meant I never got to represent Wales at any of the junior levels. From that point on I didn't get injured until I was 32. I remember I missed one game when I was at Villa with chickenpox – but that was it until I pulled a hamstring at 32. I was really lucky. Even when I moved from Derby to Liverpool I played 70 consecutive games for them in my first season there.'

October 1988 and early in the Rams' second season back in the top flight, Arthur Cox's side had won just two of their opening eight games when Saunders bounced in from Oxford United and immediately captured the imagination of the Derby faithful with two goals on his debut in a 4–1 win over Wimbledon at the Baseball Ground. Just as Kevin Hector had blown Rams fans away two decades earlier, the new star striker with speed, flair and an eye for goal became an instant crowd favourite. Goals in each of his first four games and an ability to frighten defenders as the Rams took fifth place in that campaign confirmed that Cox had unearthed a real gem.

A gem, which, only three seasons before, had been cast aside by Swansea manager John Bond. Blind to how brightly Dean might shine, Bond pushed him out on loan to Cardiff City before letting him go for free to Brighton. Oxford United snapped him up in March 1987, and 18 months later this Welsh wizard was at Derby and, aged 24, at the height of his powers. 'When I look back now at John Bond's decision to let me go, I think it's a shame for Swansea – not a shame for me,' says Dean. 'It was one man's opinion, and I use that experience now when I talk to young players. So many of them are released at 18, and I know how they feel, but I tell them not to worry. I tell them I went from one end of the scale to the other – from free transfer to record signing.

'I tell them to go away and do the business in the lower Leagues

Dean Saunders.

Deano tussles with Manchester United's Bryan Robson.

Receiving the Player of the Year award from Arthur Cox.

Dean Saunders celebrates yet another goal with Derby County supporters.

and come back and haunt the club who let you go. I was getting £60 a week at Swansea and scored 12 goals in the equivalent of the Championship at 19 – there was no need to give me a free transfer.'

Despite his natural goalscoring talent, Dean credits Arthur Cox for developing him as a player. 'Arthur made me believe in myself – he gave me the confidence,' he says. 'My dad was a footballer and was a big influence in my attitude towards work and how to live off the pitch, but it was Arthur who made me believe I could score goals against anyone. He built me up so much sometimes I thought he was talking about someone else, but everything he said to me stayed in my head. Some of the things he told me didn't make any sense to me at the time, but then I would click on.

'Roy McFarland was Arthur's sidekick, and as a world-class defender he gave me tips as well, but it was Arthur who sat next to me in the half-hour before kick-off, just saying little things to me like, "Dean, you are going to be clean through twice today so remember their goalkeeper goes down early…" And that's what would happen, and when I was in on goal Arthur's words would come back to me and I'd finish the job properly.'

He has his favourite goals of course. 'I remember my first for Derby against Wimbledon – a diving header – then there was the volley against Man City that dipped over Tony Coton and a special one too at Highbury, but my favourite was the first because you want to get off to good start,' he says. 'Derby is a great football city, and it's really where I made my mark. The Baseball Ground was special because the supporters were so close to the pitch. I used to love playing towards the Normanton End. The kids were down that end, and it really did feel like the crowd was sucking the ball into the net.

'You could hear everything the crowd said. In fact I recall one game there when, for some reason, Brian Clough, who was managing Forest at the time, was in the crowd. I slid into the boards trying to make a tackle, and all I could hear was his inimitable voice shouting at me to get up! Actually, Cloughie tried to sign me before I went to Liverpool.'

Top scorer in each of his three seasons and Player of the Year in his last campaign with the Rams, Dean and his big-name colleague Mark Wright were sacrificed after relegation for Cox's side in 1990–91. Arsenal were champions and the Rams finished bottom with 24 points, enduring a record-breaking 20 League games without a win. Still Saunders somehow recorded 20 goals in all competitions, including a hat-trick in a home draw with Sunderland. After a campaign during which Derby were unable to buy or even sign loan players, the record incoming fee of £2.9 million for Saunders (a British domestic record at the time) was used to run the wretched Robert Maxwell out of town.

Despite an FA Cup-winners' medal with Liverpool in 1992, Deano looked happier with himself in three season at Aston Villa, during which time he scored two goals in helping Villa to League Cup Final victory over Manchester United in 1994.

Seventy-five Welsh caps (22 goals) confirm his status in a game he loves so much that he went on to ply his trade with the likes of Galatasaray, Forest, Sheffield United and Bradford City before turning to coaching as part of Graeme Souness's backroom team at Blackburn and Newcastle.

His ultimate aim remains football management. 'I have learned a lot from the managers I have worked with – the likes of Arthur, Ron Atkinson, John Toshack and during my five years as coach for Graeme at Blackburn and Newcastle,' he says. 'So far as coaching goes it was a big shock for me going from playing to a completely

An unusually sombre Dean Saunders is introduced to the media by manager Arthur Cox after signing for the Rams.

Dean Saunders outpaces Paul McGrath in the Rams' 2–0 defeat by Aston Villa at the Baseball Ground in September 1990.

different world – but my enthusiasm for football is my biggest strength as a coach as well. I have done my Pro Licence, and sooner or later I must go it alone. The reason I turned down a few management jobs when I finished playing was to give myself a bigger chance of success. I needed more experience. I had seen what happened to the likes of Chris Waddle who took on Burnley too early and never got another chance.'

Dean especially enjoyed playing at Pride Park Stadium in a benefit game for his old mate Ted McMinn in an ex-Rams side managed Arthur Cox. 'Even then I had to try my best. Whenever I slow down I end up having a nightmare and, besides, the people of Derby remember me at my best so I definitely didn't want them to see me limping around Pride Park', he says...still smiling.

1991–92 **Ted McMinn**

There is no better way to endear yourself to Derby County fans than scoring one of the finest goals ever seen at the Baseball Ground on your home debut. In reality, however, even without that corker of a strike against Manchester United on 10 February 1988 Ted McMinn would still have become one of the most popular players ever to wear a Rams shirt. He played his football at a time when repartee between the fans and the players was still a part of the entertainment – and if you played on the wing like Ted did, there was no hiding place from the Popside or the Paddocks below the Main ABC Stand. Either you embraced the 'banter', as it is called today, or you sank without trace. The sanitised stadia that replaced the Baseball Ground and other relics of the past removed the bonhomie. Safety regulations mean there's at least a running track's width between the touchline and the first row of seats, and something special has been lost.

McMinn arrived almost as an after-thought in February 1988, more than halfway through Derby's first season back in the big time under Arthur Cox. The campaign had begun with the much-heralded capture of Southampton's two England internationals Peter Shilton and Mark Wright, but still the Rams were struggling to adapt to life at the top.

Ted McMinn.

That home debut game against Manchester United – McMinn's first appearance had been a 2–1 defeat at Portsmouth four days earlier – was Derby's eighth loss in a row, equalling an unwanted 23-year-old record. The sale of Bobby Davison to Leeds United before the end of 1987 had left Cox's side bereft of a target man, and it mattered not that Nigel Callaghan, who played every game that season, later in tandem with Ted, supplied good quality ball from the flanks. Young Phil Gee had no suitable partner to help him out down the middle until the belated arrival of the veteran Frank Stapleton for the final 10 games of the campaign, by which time McMinn was having a hernia fixed.

Cox had first enquired about McMinn while managing Newcastle as the young winger cut his teeth at Queen of the South. But Ted landed a dream move to Rangers still aged only 22. 'When Rangers came in for me everything else went out of the window,' Ted tells me. 'I'd moved up the ladder, and Arthur wasn't really on my radar again until I left Ibrox for Seville.'

Ted McMinn evades a tackle in the Rams' 2–0 win against Charlton Athletic at The Valley in September 1991.

Ted followed his Rangers manager Jock Wallace to Spain but was not happy during his 13 months abroad. 'It was made public that I was homesick and wanted to come back, and that's when Arthur showed his interest,' says Ted. 'Newcastle, then managed by Willie McFaul, were also still keen, and because of the way he had left Newcastle Arthur was absolutely determined that I shouldn't go there.'

Derby were so intent on landing their man that director Stuart Webb, who four years earlier had engineered the club's survival by acquiring the necessary funding to see off a High Court winding-up petition, flew out to Seville to talk business with the engaging Scot. 'That was great because although a few clubs had expressed an interest Derby were the ones willing to get off their backsides and come across and talk to me and sell the club,' says Ted. 'Mr Webb and his wife came out, and there were two or three days where I veered between Derby and Newcastle, but the thing that changed my mind was when Arthur phoned me in my hotel room. It was the first contact I'd ever had with Arthur, and when I spoke to him I decided that was the person I wanted to work for. He was just the same as Jock (Wallace) – army type and no bulls**t. He told me what he wanted and sold the club to me in the space of two or three sentences. That was my mind made up, and the hardest thing then was to go back to Newcastle and tell them I was going to Derby!'

Arguably the Rams' least media-friendly manager, Cox inspired tremendous loyalty among his players, and Ted explains: 'Arthur never publicly criticised his players, but he never doled out any praise either. The best I ever got was a tap on the shoulder and a wink; then he'd walk off. But you knew he was happy with what you'd done. He'd also be happy to give you a rollicking to your face and tell you what you hadn't done well, but to me he was a fantastic manager who helped me a lot both on and off the field. He knew my background, and he wasn't just a manager, he was a true friend, and we still talk to each other on the phone. I had a lot of ups and downs at Derby with injuries, but Arthur would always come in first thing in the morning to see how I was getting on.'

It was not only the Derby crowd McMinn had to convince as a £300,000 signing. 'I'd just played in the top League in Spain, but apart from Shilts and Wrighty I was hardly joining a team of household names,' he says. 'I think George Williams, who played for Wales, was the only other international, so they were probably looking at me when I arrived thinking "Who's he?" and I was thinking exactly the same. Playing for Rangers wasn't a big thing down in England. It's strange signing for a new club because the first thing you do is size everybody up. I wasn't a big signing as such, but luckily I picked up a good relationship with Wrighty and settled in very quickly.

124

'It was a good time of the season for me to bed in and get to know the players. To be truthful I would never have signed for Derby if I'd seen the Baseball Ground first! When they took me out onto the pitch for the first time there wasn't a blade of grass to be seen, and I'd just come from Spain and playing at the big stadiums in Barcelona and Real Madrid where you were performing on the equivalent of bowling greens. But as soon as I played my first game there, and it happened to be against Man United, I realised that 20,000 people in the Baseball Ground could make just as much noise as 100,000 in one of the super stadiums in Spain. The fans were on top of you, and luckily for me we just clicked and I enjoyed playing there – even being touched on the shoulders by the fans when I was taking a corner or a throw-in. They could bear-hug you by the corner flags!

'In that first home game I think we had everything – rain, sleet, snow on a cold February night, and I remember we were 2–0 down, and I got the ball on the halfway line and just started running. I knew the final whistle wasn't far away, and I cut inside and had a left-foot shot and as soon as it connected with my boot I knew it wasn't going to be too far away. The ball just kept climbing towards the goal and then I heard the roar. All I could think of was running after the ball to try to get it back to the halfway line for the re-start, but there wasn't enough time. It was certainly a big thing for me to get the fans on my side, and it is a goal that people keep going on about. They say it's one of the best they've seen, and it was probably the best I ever scored, but it was for nothing.'

Equally comfortable on either wing, McMinn, who soon earned himself the nickname of 'Tin Man' because of his unorthodox straight-legged running style, played the game with a smile on his face. 'People used to criticise me on the Monday morning after games and ask why I walked about the pitch smiling and talking to fans. Some of them reckoned that I couldn't be concentrating properly on my game, but I felt better having the banter with the fans. Believe me, when you weren't playing particularly well and there was no crowd noise you could hear every comment that was flying at you, and I'd turn around and have a bit of banter back and 99 per cent of the fans would laugh back at me. I was lucky enough in my career to

A typical pose from winger McMinn in the 1992–93 season.

Ted McMinn scores in the Rams' 5–0 win over Cambridge United in the Littlewoods Cup at the Baseball Ground in October 1989. The Rams won 6–2 on aggregate to move into the third round.

have that sort of relationship with the fans. I played with a smile on my face, which you don't see nowadays because modern-day players are like robots. I preferred the players of the past like Paul Gascoigne and Jim Baxter, who had a bit of personality.

'The two grounds I liked playing at best were the Baseball Ground and Loftus Road. I remember being put over the wall by a slide tackle once at Queen's Park Rangers and it was exactly the same at the Baseball Ground when Trevor Putney had a go at me and big Wrighty put him in row C when Derby played Norwich. But those grounds were nice and compact, unlike the majority of stadiums now where the players are separated from the crowd. Everything has moved on and everything has got bigger.'

Just seven games into his Derby County career McMinn was packed off to Harley Street with injured full-back Mel Sage for a hernia operation that would ensure he was fighting fit for the start of the 1988–89 campaign, which would go down as the Rams' best effort in recent times. 'I trained through the summer with (club physio) Gordon Guthrie so I was ready for pre-season, and I was really buzzing because I'd come from Spain and I was desperate to prove myself,' Ted recalls. 'That season we beat Man United and Arsenal at their grounds – it was incredible. Early on we went to Forest, and I remember we came away with a draw, and me and Wrighty were in the car going down to Oxford and we agreed that we could have a good season. We still didn't have any really big names, but as a team we worked very hard together, and Dean Saunders arrived and lifted the dressing room. He's just one of the most bubbly guys I have ever met. He could talk the talk and walk the walk. He came in and put a smile on everyone's face. He's a chirpy wee Welsh lad who was just great to be around.'

Another striker, Paul Goddard, had already arrived from Newcastle United in the summer of 1988. 'He was completely different,' says Ted, 'a quiet lad, and a real gentleman. But for a wide man Saunders and Goddard were just a dream to play with. They weren't the tallest in terms of being target men, but when the ball went up there Dean especially could jump and time it well, and Paul was strong and could hold it up. So we had me on one side and Gary Micklewhite on the other, and it was a great combination. We ended up fifth, which would usually have got us into Europe, but for the ban on English clubs after Heysel.

'Will Derby ever make it to fifth in the top League again? Sadly I would have to say no because the top six teams now are so strong. But that season we believed in each other, and we thought with a few more signings we would be able to step on again if Mr Maxwell had decided to spend his money. Of course we know now he never had any money to spend in the first place!'

McMinn scored four times in 38 League and Cup appearances that season, and as the following campaign got underway the winger who delighted in taking on full-backs and leaving them on their backsides was playing so well an international call-up for Scotland's 1990 World Cup adventure was very much on the cards. However, then came a career-threatening injury in a 2–1 victory at Tottenham on 25 November 1989. 'That was the low-point of my career because I was on fire and playing probably more consistently than at any other time in my career,' he recalls. 'It's just something that can happen in football. I never seemed to get wee niggly injuries like hamstrings or calf strains, with me it was always a big thing! My whole knee collapsed and ripped, and I left White Hart Lane on crutches to be taken up to the DRI [Derbyshire Royal Infirmary]. I saw the surgeon there who operated first thing the following morning. I think Arthur was one of the few people around me at that time who thought I would play again. It was a big blow for me, especially with the World Cup coming up.

Ted leaving Rangers for Derby on a charity bike ride shortly after having his right leg amputated.

'It took 14 months to get over it, six months at Lilleshall followed by eight months at Derby County, and other little injuries cropped up such as the pin that was holding the knee together working loose and at one stage my cartilage snapped, but I got chucked in the following January in what was almost a relegation battle against Vinny Jones at Sheffield United. My knee had a big white bandage on it to protect it, which wasn't a good idea because I think it just attracted opponents to hit that left leg. My knee was never really right again, and Vinny Jones certainly tested it out within the first two minutes, but I got through the game.

'It's fair to say I'd perhaps lost a yard of pace

but that was because I'd lost a lot of flexibility in the leg. In any case I wasn't going to chuck it in. Tin Man? There were certainly a lot of things rattling inside my left leg by that time, and I was always in pain. The doctor told me I couldn't play two games inside seven days because I was getting so much fluid above the knee. There's no way I would have walked away just because of a bit of pain, because what I would have done anyway away from football?'

Even a returning McMinn could not prevent relegation in 1991, but the Tin Man's greatest triumph was to come the following season, after Wright and Saunders had departed for Liverpool, when the fans voted him Player of the Year in a third-placed finish in the old Division Two. 'Arthur took a big gamble in 1991–92 because he played me in the middle more and also gave me the captain's armband when George (Williams) got injured which was an honour. I felt four inches taller leading the team out. We had a fantastic run towards the end of the season and although I heard the whispers about me not being as good as I'd been before the injury, I played a lot of games and we got into the Play-offs.'

Ted played a total of 43 League and Cup games that season, including both legs of the Play-off semi-final against Blackburn Rovers. At Ewood Park Cox's team threw away a two-goal advantage, losing 4–2, and a 2–1 victory at the Baseball Ground three days later was not enough. 'Getting the Player of the Year award at the end of the season was a fantastic achievement after Wrighty had won it two seasons on the trot and then Dean Saunders,' says Ted. 'Receiving the Jack Stamps Trophy on the pitch before the last game was amazing. We could have won promotion that day, but we got into the Play-offs and losing to Blackburn was so demoralising because all I could think was how hard I had worked all season but at the end it was worth nothing.

'I knew that season would probably be my last as a regular because new players, Marco Gabbiadini, Paul Simpson and Tommy Johnson had started to come in. Tommy was definitely coming in to fill my position.'

The Derby crowd were treated only to cameo appearances from the popular winger in a disappointing 1992–93 campaign, and in the summer of '93 he was on his way to Birmingham City for an unhappy spell before enjoying himself again at Burnley, where he found a connection with the Turf Moor crowd.

Mark Wright's assistant manager at Southport, Oxford United and Chester from 2000 to 2002, McMinn had part of his right leg amputated because of a mystery infection in 2005 but bounced back in typical Tin Man style on an artificial leg, one so effective that he was able to take part in a marathon charity bike ride soon after his recovery. His popularity as a Derby player was underlined when a record Pride Park attendance of 33,475 turned out for his benefit game between Derby and Rangers legends on 1 May 2006. 'The place was bouncing that day and I think the occasion will stick in people's minds,' he says. 'The Derby fans will hopefully remember a great day and the Rangers fans will still be wondering how they got to Derby in the first place! They were that drunk!

'It's strange being a supporter at Pride Park now because I sit with the fans and hear the comments and people always turn around and ask me what I think. I feel lucky to be an ex-player and I love mixing with the fans because Derby County supporters are absolutely fantastic. That's probably why I've never moved away from Derby and that's the case with so many former Derby players. This is the place that feels like home.'

1992–93 **Marco Gabbiadini**

When the time comes to hang up the shooting boots after an illustrious career, some ex-pros are cute enough to admit that any other job in football just cannot compare with the adrenaline rush of playing the beautiful game. It is one of the reasons that, rather than screaming at the latest generation of players from the touchline dug-out, Marco Gabbiadini is more likely to be found welcoming unsuspecting guests to the sumptuous Bishops Hotel in York.

Marco and wife Deborah are proprietors of the award-winning Victorian villa, and while Mrs Gabbiadini's claim that Marco has swapped his boots for a pair of marigolds does not quite ring true, Bishops Hotel guests are likely to see a man who banged in 68 goals for the Rams in 200 starts busying himself around the place.

'We have Derby and Sunderland fans as guests having picked the hotel out on the internet not knowing we run the place and their reactions can be quite bizarre,' Marco tells me. 'At first there are a lot of double takes because they recognise my face but can't quite place me in a different context. Of course there are others who book especially because they know it's our place, and that's great.'

While the likes of Paul Simpson, a close mate from Derby County's promotion-winning side of 1996, continued their careers into football management, Marco has turned his back on the game – for the time being. 'Simmo went out and got all his coaching badges, but being a manager or coach is a full-on commitment,' he says. 'The main reason I've chosen to do something different is my family.

'There's no job like being a professional footballer, and I was lucky enough to have played the game for 20 years. It's a great way to earn a living. In my book, coaching and managing simply can't compare with playing. Although it's the same industry, football management is a proper job that demands time and commitment. Playing is different. You get plenty of time to spend with your family, and probably the only downside is having to move around. That's why, when my

Marco Gabbiadini.

Marco gets in a shot against Charlton Athletic at the Baseball Ground in October 1992. The Rams won 4–3.

playing days were over, I decided I didn't want to be nomadic any more. I wanted to be master of my own destiny.

'We needed to do something of course because I wasn't able to live off my time as a player, so we chose the hotel trade. To start with, I thought we had created a monster because we had absolutely no time to ourselves. But we stuck with it, did well, employed staff and live off-site now, which makes life more pleasant.'

So is the Gabbiadini hotel empire set to go global? Marco laughs. 'We do look at it sometimes and feel we could run a bigger place for the same amount of effort, but we both value family life and won't do anything rash until the kids are more independent.'

Marco has three daughters; Amelia, Evangelina and Liliana and a son, Jules. It is Jules, a prolific striker with York City's junior sides in recent years, who is dragging Marco back into football. 'Happily, although he's a striker, he's not going to be directly compared with me,' says Marco, 'because he's taller with a nice touch. I was more raw power!'

Watching Jules play takes Marco back to his time at the same club as a kid. Born in Nottingham – his Italian-born dad worked on the National Grid and was based in Derby for a time – Marco grew up in York and, despite his football prowess, was always urged by his parents to make the most of his academic talents. 'I never did any of the academy stuff,' he says. 'As a kid I went to Notts County on and off in the holidays when Jimmy Sirrell was there and then Middlesbrough every now and again, but I didn't live for football. I did fairly well academically and went to grammar school in York. I stayed on to do A-levels, but things started to get a bit difficult when I had to leave school early to play for York reserves. Eventually I became the last-ever professionally contracted apprentice when I signed for York in 1985.'

A promising goals record in his first 50 starts for York saw Marco selected for England Under-18s – the powers that be at the FA were keen they got to this dually qualified striker before the Italians! But it was at Sunderland that the headline-writers' dream player ('Marco Goalo!') burst onto the scene. Still only 19, he moved to the North East for £80,000 when York City boss Denis Smith was appointed to the hot seat at Roker Park. 'Sunderland were at their lowest ebb when I went there,' says Marco. 'They'd just been relegated into the old Third Division, but it was always a big setup. I teamed up with Eric Gates, who was a veteran by then but still a great player, and we managed to get promoted in my first year. My time at Sunderland and Derby were definitely my best years.'

The goals flowed over the next four seasons as he helped Sunderland into the top flight and earned England Under-21 and England B honours before being transferred to Crystal Palace for a club record £1.8 million in October 1991. Just three months later, after enduring a miserable time at Selhurst Park, Marco was rescued by the Rams for £1 million as Arthur Cox began to spend Lionel Pickering's huge investment in the club. 'If Derby hadn't come in for me I probably would have stayed,' he says. 'I think I scored five goals in 15 appearances for Palace, which wasn't bad, but I had a nagging knee injury which meant I was never 100 per cent fit there. So it didn't work out, but I was impressed by Derby's ambition and was happy to make the switch.'

Do not mention the Play-offs to Marco. At Sunderland he lost in the Final to Swindon Town, though the Black Cats eventually benefited from the Wiltshire club's disqualification, and in his first

Marco takes the ball past a defender, watched by Martin Kuhl, in the Rams' 5–0 win over Sunderland at the Baseball Ground on the opening day of the 1993–94 season.

Gabbiadini in high–flying action in the Rams' 1–0 defeat by Sunderland at the Baseball Ground in April 1995.

season at Derby there was disappointment in the two-leg Play-off semi against Blackburn. 'We were 2–0 up in the Ewood Park leg and ended up losing 4–2 and were winning the home leg 2–0 when Kevin Moran somehow shouldered a winner for Blackburn,' he says. 'It was a nightmare. Two seasons later we went to the Play-off Final at Wembley and lost to Leicester when we should have won. I think John Harkes missed one from about a yard out that day. Even when I went to Darlington at the end of my career I lost in the Play-off Final…so please don't invite me to the game if ever Derby get involved again!'

Player of the Year in his second season with the Rams, Marco eventually enjoyed promotion to the Premiership in 1995–96 but cannot explain why a side put together on a shoe-string through Jim Smith's wily wheeler-dealing succeeded where Arthur Cox's multi-million pound spending had failed. 'Jim came in, and although the playing staff did not change dramatically there were some important additions,' Marco recalls. 'Vanders [Robin Van Der Laan] came in as captain, and the likes of Gary Rowett, a youngster who was perceived as a make-weight in Craig Short's transfer to Everton, turned out to be a top player.

'Igor [Stimac] arrived in November, and then of course there was Steve McClaren, an unknown quantity at the time, who was a great coach for the players. Whatever anyone says about Steve now, even after his time as the boss of the England team, his method in his Derby days was terrific. I enjoyed what we did on the training ground, and although a lot of people thought of Jim as being old school he embraced the new techniques and let Steve run with the scientific approach to football that was coming in at that time.

'My favourite game was the pre-Christmas fixture at the Baseball Ground against Sunderland. We needed to win to go top at their expense, and because Vanders was out injured Jim asked me to captain the side. I scored, we won, went top, and it was one of those fantastic atmospheres at the Baseball Ground.'

But the proprietor of York's Bishops Hotel has work to do. 'We have a nice life,' he muses, 'but if I'm honest I am starting to miss the football. Having played the game non-stop all those years, I've enjoyed the break from that level of commitment, but watching Jules is getting me going again. He's a bright boy so we try to encourage him with his schoolwork, just like my parents did with me, but if he can crack it, well…I'd love him to do it because being a footballer is every kid's dream job.'

1993–94 **Martin Taylor**

It was the summer of 1995, my first day in the press office at the Baseball Ground, and the welcoming party consisted of Martin Taylor…on crutches. Propped up outside the Ramtique shop, his left leg in plaster, he looked cheerful enough, but I knew, as did he, that this young goalkeeper, once tipped to follow Peter Shilton into the England team, might never play again.

Nine months earlier the Rams' reigning Player of the Year had sustained an horrendous double fracture of his left leg when courage got the better of him in a rough-and-tumble encounter at Southend's Roots Hall. The injury looked so bad a surgeon gently enquired of him in hospital whether he had been involved in a motorbike accident. In fact he'd been hit by a steam train in the shape of Southend striker Dave Regis. Taylor's pain was broadcast live to a Sunday TV audience together with the 4,214 faithful who turned up at Roots Hall that October afternoon.

All the talk was of Taylor's courage. Not only had he dived in at Regis's feet, somehow, even after the sickening collision, Derby's goalkeeper had managed to crawl to the loose ball and push it beyond the by-line to safety.

'It was 0–0, just after half-time,' Martin tells me. 'We had a corner and it was cleared. Regis received the ball just outside our box and knocked it into the area. I dived at his feet and got the ball, and his knee got my leg. Immediately I was in sheer agony, so much so that I let the ball go. Why I crawled to knock it out for a corner I don't know – just instinct I suppose.

'Bruce (Michael Forsyth) was there straight away and told me not to move. Then Gordy (physio

Martin Taylor receives the Player of the Year award from Roy McFarland.

Martin is stretchered from the Roots Hall pitch.

Gordon Guthrie) came to have a look at me, and the next thing I knew I was in the changing room waiting for an ambulance. I had a chesty cough at the time so they wouldn't give me a general anaesthetic for the operation – it had to be an epidural. The op lasted five hours and I was out of it most of the time, but I do remember waking up at one point and hearing a clunking noise and seeing a surgeon literally hammering a nail into my leg!'

Although no one told Martin directly that he would never play again, the writing was on the wall when, the day after Jim Smith arrived as Rams manager in that summer of 1995, the 'keeper had to undergo a second operation. His shattered leg simply hadn't healed properly the first time around. Attempts to bridge a 10mm gap in his shinbone had failed. 'Jim must have taken one look at me and decided I would never play again, and I can't blame him for that,' says Martin. However, throughout a distinguished career, Martin Taylor made a habit out of proving the doubters wrong.

Brought up in Tamworth, he was always a goalkeeper, just like his father and brother before him. Spotted playing for Mile Oak Rovers by Derby County's chief scout Ron Jukes, Martin arrived at the Baseball Ground in the summer of 1986, a raw 20-year-old, third choice in the pecking order behind Mark Wallington and Eric Steele. Arthur Cox was the manager, and Derby had just won promotion after a couple of seasons in the Division Three doldrums. 'There were no goalkeeping coaches in those days – you just worked with the other 'keepers and hopefully picked up good habits from them,' says Martin.

No bad thing then when arguably the greatest England 'keeper of them all – Peter Shilton – arrived for the 1987–88 campaign as Cox guided Derby back into the top flight with consecutive promotions. 'Working with Shilts was a dream come true. I have to admit Bruce Grobbelar was my favourite goalkeeper as a kid, but being on the same training ground as the best in the world...well, if you can't learn from Shilts you can't learn from anyone. It's not that he made a special effort with me, but we trained together and if I asked him how to handle a particular situation he would give me advice. That was his way – he never said "You must do it like this..." he simply told me the way he did things and let me make up my own mind.

'Even near the end of his time at Derby his reputation was such that in shooting practice a striker had to do something out of the ordinary to beat him. He still had a presence about him that put pressure on opponents.'

In his first two seasons Shilton did not miss a game, though those in the know were talking about the understudy waiting in the wings who might one day take over as England's number one. 'I went on loan to Carlise and Scunthorpe to gain experience, and the reserve League in those days was also a good standard, so I kept my hand in. My debut was a League Cup quarter-final replay against West Ham at the Baseball Ground in 1990. I think Shilts had cut his eye playing for England, so I finally got my chance. It finished 0–0, and I didn't have a shot to save, but I kept a clean sheet.

'I was proud to finally get in. You train week in week out for that, and the Baseball Ground was always a special place – it had such a tremendous atmosphere.'

Unfortunately Shilton and injuries were rare bedfellows, and by the time the goalkeeping legend played his last game for the Rams in February 1992 Martin had chalked up only a dozen appearances in six seasons. 'When Shilts left Arthur told me in the morning I would get my chance – and in the afternoon he signed Steve Sutton from Forest! The team was going for the Play-offs, and I think Arthur felt it was too much to ask me to step up.'

Still, Martin was given four games as Derby's number one immediately post-Shilton, one of which was a 4–3 defeat at Tranmere Rovers. 'We were 3–1 up in that game and I made a mistake. Graham Richards, commentating for *BBC Radio Derby*, described it as "a mistake of inter-galactic proportions". I felt ridiculed, and some people even blamed me for us not getting promoted that season.

'That spurred me on to prove people wrong, and it was especially sweet for me when the fans voted me their Player of the Season in 1994.'

Season 1992–93 saw the introduction of the back-pass rule, and it was the break Martin needed. A fine footballer who was equally comfortable kicking with either foot, he was given his chance halfway through the campaign and embarked on a run of 78 consecutive League appearances. 'Being two-footed was to my advantage, because Sutty (Steve Sutton) struggled for a time and lost confidence. Eric Steele came back to the club as goalkeeping coach around that time, and he was the best coach I worked with. Goalkeepers nowadays have to be all-round footballers. When I first started it was fine for a 'keeper to dive in at strikers' feet, but these days if you touch them you give away a penalty and you are off.'

Despite the disappointment of a Wembley Play-off defeat at the hands of Leicester, season 1993–

Craig Short, Mickey Forsyth, Martin Taylor and Gary Charles look concerned as Millwall fans invade the pitch after the Rams' 3–1 defeat of Millwall in the First Division play-off semi-final second leg at The Den in May 1994.

Martin returns to action in the FA Cup against Middlesbrough.

94 was the highlight of Martin's career. Not only was he an ever present (the last Derby player to achieve this feat) with 53 League and Cup appearances, he was Player of the Year. 'I had been runner-up the year before, and it was brilliant to get the fans' vote, especially after the criticism I had faced two seasons before. Unfortunately, the Leicester game left us all feeling empty. We were a few minutes away from playing in the Premiership, and losing was a major disappointment because we dominated the game.'

Fourteen games into the next campaign Martin's career shuddered to a halt at Roots Hall.

The press office at the Baseball Ground was situated under the main stand, and a familiar sound from above was the thump-thump of trainers on wooden steps – up and down, up and down, with words of encouragement from Gordon Guthrie. This was Martin Taylor, determined to get back to fitness, but he was the Rams' forgotten man as Jim Smith guided the club to the Premiership for the first time and Russell Hoult grabbed the number-one jersey, making it his own.

A few eyebrows were raised when at the turn of the new year in 1997 Martin started playing again for the reserves – and then Hoult suffered a fit of the jitters that culminated in a 6–1 mauling at Middlesbrough's Riverside in the March. Three days later the Rams were due to meet Boro again in the quarter-final of the FA Cup at the Baseball Ground, and manager Smith decided he could not risk Hoult. Twenty-three months after being laid low at Southend, Martin Taylor was back as number one.

I well recall the feeling in the Baseball Ground crowd that day; every Rams fan was nervous for the comeback kid, willing him to do well. 'To be honest I was still learning what my leg could and couldn't do, like jumping off both legs for crosses,' Martin recalls. 'I had to turn myself into a different 'keeper – it was all about learning to keep goal again. I knew I could do it, but I suppose I went into that Boro game 80 per cent certain.'

Martin could not be blamed for either of the Boro goals as Bryan Robson's side marched on into the semis to play Chesterfield. And he was back, playing in a 1–0 defeat at Everton and then in an impressive 4–2 home win over Tottenham. In his testimonial season things were going well for Martin Taylor. Too well.

'So far as I was concerned I had the rest of the season to earn myself a new contract. I'd played in three games and done nothing wrong. I was having a round of golf at The Belfry on the Wednesday before we were due to play Manchester United at Old Trafford on the Saturday and Steve McClaren rang me and said, "How do you fancy going on loan to Wycombe"?'

Jim Smith had signed Estonian international 'keeper Mart Poom, and Martin was out in the cold again. 'I went to play for John Gregory at Wycombe, but 10 days later I was recalled because Poomy

Martin says farewell to Derby after 10 years at his testimonial game in May 1997.

Pictured before the injury.

got injured. My last match for Derby was a 0–0 draw against Forest at the Baseball Ground. I kept a clean sheet and was made Man of the Match – and that's how it finished. I wish I'd been given a real crack at it. I think Jim doubted I would last a full season, but I went on to play 300 League games after that, missing two games in six seasons – and that through suspension!'

Player of the Year in three of his six seasons at Wycombe before moving briefly to Telford United as coach and then in July 2004 to Burton Albion as player coach, Taylor is not bitter that the Roots Hall incident stunted a flourishing career. 'Yes there was talk about me following Shilts into the England team, but it's all ifs and buts. I wouldn't change anything that's happened – in fact my injury made me a better person. I appreciate things more. The one time it did hit home was when England selected Ian Walker in goal. I knew I had been a much better 'keeper than him, but that's the way it goes.'

These days Taylor, a partner in a building firm, is enjoying life and still living with his family in Findern, where he retained a home even during his time with Wycombe. 'I never moved away from Derby because it's such a great place to live,' he says. 'When I played for the Rams a 10-minute shopping trip would take two hours because everyone wanted to talk to me.

'These days it's different, and I prefer it that way. It made me smile in town the other week when I heard someone whisper to a mate, "That bloke looks just like Martin Taylor...".'

1994–95 **Craig Short**

Craig Short was the final piece in Arthur Cox's jigsaw and the last major investment of Lionel Pickering when he arrived from Notts County for a club record £2.65 million in September 1992.

After being forced to sell his best players, Mark Wright and Dean Saunders, to Liverpool the previous summer to raise the cash to buy out the hugely unpopular Robert Maxwell, Derby County were short of money until Pickering stepped in with his millions in November 1991.

Pickering, the majority shareholder but preferring at that time to adopt the role of vice-chairman, made his intentions clear by funding a series of big-money signings, starting with the £1 million acquisition of striker Marco Gabbiadini in January 1992, and followed soon afterwards by Paul Simpson (£500,000 from Oxford United), Paul Kitson (£1.3 million from Leicester City), and Tommy Johnson (£1.3 million from Notts County).

For manager Cox, who had not had a bean to spend in over three years, this was a luxury indeed, and his new signings seemed to have the desired effect as the Rams went unbeaten in the final eight games of the 1991–92 season, winning six, to claim third place in the old Second Division behind promoted Ipswich Town and Middlesbrough.

It was a major disappointment that they could not take this dazzling form into the Play-offs, where they lost in the semi-final over two legs to Blackburn Rovers, another big-spending club that was destined for top-flight glory. Despite finishing behind Derby in sixth, Rovers had taken all the points in the two League encounters that campaign.

When Cox splashed Pickering's cash again in the summer of 1992 to bring in midfielder Mark Pembridge from Luton Town, most football pundits reckoned Derby were only a commanding central-defender away from having by far the most complete squad in the re-styled Division One (this was the first year of the FA Premiership). Short was therefore the man who would make things happen,

Craig Short patrolling the back line.

138

Craig signs for the Rams in September 1992.

and it was certainly clear something was desperately missing when expectant Rams fans endured a miserable start to the 1992–93 campaign as Cox's side managed only two points from the first six games before Short made his debut at West Ham – set to win automatic promotion behind Newcastle United – in a 1–1 draw on 20 September.

Six days later, on Short's home debut, Derby finally recorded their first win of the season, Gabbiadini and Simpson scoring in a 2–0 victory over Southend United. The same two players were among the goals again in a 3–1 win at Cambridge United at the start of October, and four days later Southend United were emphatically beaten 7–0 at the Baseball Ground in the second round of the League Cup.

A late starter to League football, the Bridlington-born Short – square-jawed, powerful and organised – had played for Pickering Town and Scarborough before Notts County recognised his potential at the age of 21. A member of Neil Warnock's side that won back-to-back promotions to earn a place in the top flight in 1991, Short had played 128 League games for Notts when Cox prised him away after a brief sojourn in the top League.

Short truly demonstrated his value to his new side on the road, as between the start of October and 20 December the Rams recorded seven consecutive away wins. Still, something was not right: during the same period middling sides such as Oxford United, Millwall, Sunderland and Tranmere Rovers all won at the Baseball Ground. Derby were erratic and, while an appearance at Wembley in the Final of the Anglo-Italian Cup in March 1993 (they lost 3–1 to Cremonese) was a welcome distraction for Derby supporters, the League campaign was hugely disappointing as Cox's star-studded side finished 10 points shy of the Play-off places in eighth.

Short was one of the goalscorers as the 1993–94 campaign started in cracking style at the Baseball Ground with a 5–0 humiliation of Sunderland, but the inconsistent form of the previous campaign again haunted the Rams. They conceded three goals in defeats at Middlesbrough and Birmingham City

Craig battles with three opponents in the Rams' 2–1 defeat by Tranmere Rovers at the Baseball Ground in November 1992.

before going to Short's former club Notts County on 25 September and losing 4–1. Cox, who had been absent from the touchline with a chronic back problem, called it a day after more than nine years, handing over responsibility to Roy McFarland, assistant to both Cox and his predecessor Peter Taylor for the previous 11 years.

Although Short was on the score sheet again as Derby scored five in McFarland's first game in charge, an eight-goal thriller against West Bromwich Albion on 3 October, the Rams could do nothing throughout the campaign to chase down the two sides that claimed outright promotion, Crystal Palace and Nottingham Forest.

Despite a last-match 4–3 defeat at Southend's Roots Hall, Derby pipped Notts County to the final Play-off place, and McFarland's side overcame Millwall (and a pitch invasion at the New Den) in the two-leg semi-final to face Leicester City in the Play-off Final at Wembley on 30 May. In a role-reversal of the Final that would take place 13 years later at the new Wembley stadium, when Bill Davies's unspectacular side would have the tenacity to beat more flamboyant opponents West Brom, McFarland's team of 1994 were the better footballing side but ultimately lost out to a dogged Leicester outfit. It was agony for the long-suffering Derby supporters, who experienced the ecstasy of Tommy Johnson's 27th-minute opener, only to watch Brian Little's Leicester peg it back before half-time and scramble a heart-breaking winner three minutes from time.

Pickering, now chairman, was losing patience, and the club was losing money. McFarland was required to raise cash and somehow still maintain the promotion push in 1994–95, but the momentum had been lost. After scoring 49 goals for the Rams, Kitson – apparently at odds with strike partner Gabbiadini – joined Newcastle United for £2.25 million in September 1994, and Johnson, who scored 41, followed in the New Year in a £2.9 million two-player deal with Aston Villa that also took Gary Charles to Villa Park.

Derby again demonstrated an irritating level of inconsistency, following up a wretched February with five consecutive wins in March – a run of results that saw McFarland win the First Division's Manager of the Month award. It was not good enough, however, and with his side heading for a ninth-place finish and his contract running out the Derby County legend knew his time was up.

Craig wins the ball in the air in the Rams' 2–0 defeat by Nottingham Forest at the Baseball Ground in April 1994.

Craig Short wheels away in celebration after his goal in the 5–0 win over Sunderland at the Baseball Ground on the opening day of the 1993–94 season.

The fans knew it too, and at the last home game of the season against Southend on 29 April McFarland received a warm reception from Rams supporters as he presented the Player of the Year award to Craig Short, a model of consistency in another season of under-achievement for the team.

It was to be the last act at the Baseball Ground as Derby men for McFarland and Short – both tremendous centre-halves. Short was suspended for the game and a downbeat Derby lost 2–1 to Southend, who had a future Rams player in Chris Powell to thank for laying on one of their goals that afternoon.

By the time I joined the staff at the Baseball Ground in the summer of 1995, Jim Smith was the new manager and both Short and Pembridge had taken a short cut to the Premiership, Short joining Everton and Pembridge moving on to Sheffield Wednesday.

In an indirect way, however, Short had not made his final contribution to the Derby County cause. A young defender named Gary Rowett arrived from Everton as a makeweight in the Short deal and went on to mature in Smith's promotion-winning side of 1995–96 and during the first Premiership years. Smith also had around £2 million to play with from the transfer and used the cash to stunningly good effect as Pickering's promotion dream was finally realised.

Short, who played 143 games for Derby, scoring 13 goals, went on to clock up more than 100 appearances for Everton and was still good enough at the age of 31 to attract a £1.7 million move to Blackburn Rovers. He re-joined Neil Warnock at Sheffield United before quitting the game at the age of 38 to concentrate on the business he co-owns, Outreachsailing, which teaches sailing on Lake Windermere. Craig, who was born by the sea but claims early experiences of sailing with his mother as a kid in Whitby frightened the life out of him, says: 'I found football very pressurised, and you need something to replace that feeling you get after winning, that big competitive edge in your life.' He describes sailing the Atlantic as 'the most incredible experience of my life', adding: 'I had quite a cosseted life as a footballer, and it is something so far removed from that.'

1995–96 **Dean Yates**

There are some Derby County fans who will swear Igor Stimac was Player of the Year when Jim Smith's side won promotion to the Premiership for the first time in 1996. In fact, the charismatic Igor himself will also swear it was him! The recipient was actually one of football's nice-guys, centre-half Dean Yates who, unusually in an injury-plagued career, played 38 games that season, an appearance record in 1995–96 bettered only by goalkeeper Russell Hoult and skipper Robin van der Laan.

'I missed the last two games that season,' he tells me after a trip to the Rams' Moor Farm Training Ground to collect his young son Matthew, a promising goalkeeper. 'The first was that massive promotion decider against Crystal Palace at the Baseball Ground. We needed to win to go up, and a few days before the game we travelled to Leeds for a training camp and I managed to injure my bad knee.

'The Palace game was on the Sunday, and Jim Smith and Steve McClaren told me they'd wait until the morning of the game to see if I could get through a fitness test. It was obvious I wasn't 100 per cent, but I pleaded with Macca to at least let me start the game. The answer was no.

Dean Yates.

'So there I was by the side of the pitch with Gordon Guthrie and Martin Taylor, feeling really down in the dumps, and Jim came up to me, put his hand on my shoulder and said, "Derby fans are an honest bunch, and you're going to get a big lift today – they've voted you Player of the Year!"'

Dean will not thank me for reminding him that as he limped back down the uneven Baseball Ground tunnel that morning, he was in tears. I know, because I saw him.

'Receiving the award before kick-off in front of those fans was incredible, but not playing subdued the moment,' Dean recalls. 'I dragged my chin around the place all afternoon, even when the shout went up in the dressing room before the game that the lads were going to win it for me. They did, of course, and the rest is history.'

When Dean Yates broke into the Notts County first team at 17, experts purred about his strength and class. This, they declared, was a future England international. 'I joined Notts at 14, was

Dean Yates pictured (centre), celebrating in the 1995–96 season after scoring a goal.

taken on as an apprentice and was given my chance by Richie Barker,' he says. 'Neil Warnock eventually took us into the top flight, and I know numerous clubs were taking an interest in me.'

Almost an ever present for the preceding five seasons and by now an England Under-21 international, Dean scored Notts' first goal back in the top flight, heading the winner against Southampton in August 1991. He was on top of the world, but on his 24th birthday – 26 October – the problems started. 'We were playing at Arsenal, and it was a nothing sort of challenge, but I extended my knee a little and something went. I had treatment, came back and collapsed again. Eventually my cruciate ruptured completely. I missed the next two years.'

Barely a month back into first-team football, Dean was approached by Rams manager Roy McFarland. It was January 1995, and the legendary former centre-half was willing to take a gamble on Dean to perk up another middling sort of season at the Baseball Ground. 'Roy was brilliant,' says Dean. 'He convinced me he wanted me to come to the club. The fee went to tribunal eventually.'

Roy Mac knew that if Dean could get back to anything like the player he had been before injury struck he had bagged a real bargain at £350,000. 'I was a bit gutted when Jim Smith arrived that summer because I only played half a season under Roy,' says Dean. 'Roy had been one of the best centre-halves in the world, and I could have learned loads from him, but Jim came in and reminded me a lot of one of my early influences in football, Jimmy Sirrell. He was totally honest.'

Asked about the inspirational Igor, who arrived at Derby at the end of October 1995, and Dean grins. 'Everyone remembers his first game away at Tranmere – our hopes were high and we got smashed 5–1. We played a flat back four that day, and Igor was absolutely awful. He was all over the place, out of position and hopeless. But Jim was canny. He brought in Gary Rowett to partner me in central-defence and left Igor as the spare man. Jim talked about a sweeper system but in reality we still played a flat back four and ignored Igor – we just let him do whatever he wanted to do in front of us!'

In the Premiership for the first time and playing their last season at the Baseball Ground, the Rams kicked-off at home against Leeds in a 3–3 thriller in which the injury jinx struck again for Dean. 'I took a knock in that game and didn't feature again until the home win over Leicester in the November,' he says. 'Jim had brought in Paul McGrath to shore up the defence, and he was quality – a great defender, so it was difficult to get into the side.'

By the middle of the next campaign – season 1997–98 – Dean was almost the forgotten man of a Rams squad now playing at Pride Park Stadium. 'I didn't really make my mark until the December when we travelled to Newcastle and drew 0–0,' he says. 'We had loads of injures and I came in at the back alongside young Steve Elliott, who I think was making his debut.'

Dean's consistent performances made him a difficult player to leave out, and he enjoyed a great run in the team. It finished abruptly in the 1–0 home defeat at the hands of Aston Villa on 7 February 1998.

The antics that afternoon of Villa's twin strikers Dwight Yorke and Stan Collymore will live long in the memories of the Rams faithful. 'I remember putting in an early challenge on Collymore – a fair one – that sent him spinning in the air,' says Dean. 'When he landed he turned to me and said, "Don't you ever do that to me again." I simply told him if the ball was there for me to take he would get another one. That's the clean version! It was

Dean lifts the Centenary Cup after victory over Chesterfield.

Dean in action at Pride Park Stadium.

a good 25 minutes after that when Yorke, that happy, smiling footballer everyone knows and loves, hit me late. Very late. I played the ball and I saw him coming, but I couldn't get out of the way and I felt the pain in my right ankle.

'I heard from those who saw what happened next, including my two brothers, that Collymore and Yorke seemed to congratulate each other as I was lying in agony.'

That was it. Dean Yates never played for Derby again and that summer was given a free transfer to Watford. 'I wanted to see out my career at Derby, but Jim pulled me into his office and said he had to be fair to the club and let me go. I signed a three-year contract with Watford, but the knee went again on a training camp at Lilleshall. There was really nothing they could do this time and I eventually quit in 2000.'

These days Dean works as a summariser for BBC Radio Nottingham at Notts County games…and as a taxi service for his three children.

Looking back, does he ever wonder what might have been if he had stayed injury-free? 'As a kid I dreamed of playing in the top flight and representing my country,' he says. 'I did it at Under-21 level and played 100-odd games in the top League, so I try to tell myself I was bloody lucky. But yes, sometimes I think, "What if…".'

1996–97 **Chris Powell**

He has been described as quite possibly the nicest man in football. Insiders who wax lyrical about the communication skills of Chris Powell are pretty much bang on the mark.

Jim Smith's promotion-winning side was well into a 20–match unbeaten run in the League when Chris arrived in the January of 1996 for £750,000 from Southend United. Introduced to the Derby public at a Baseball Ground press conference, the new signing promised the assembled media: 'Win, lose or draw, I'll always talk to you. I won't hide.' He was as good as his word over the next two-and-a-half years before being curiously off-loaded to Charlton Athletic, prematurely written off by manager Smith at the age of only 28.

In my job as a football club press officer footballers impressed not so much by their performances on the field of play but more by how helpful and community-minded they were off it. So it used to pain me, for example, when Lee Carsley, another of football's 'nice' people, took stick from the Baseball Ground crowd during his Derby days. It just did not seem fair. Compare this with the hero-worship adorned on such as Igor Stimac, a charismatic leader on the field of play but often surly and, at best, charmingly unhelpful off it.

Chris Powell – typically with a smile on his face.

When the likes of Lee Carsley, Chrissy Powell or, in more recent times, Marc Edworthy, put in great displays and even banged in a goal (remember Carso's in the Pride Park trouncing of Southampton and Chrissy's at home against Everton?) the pleasure was intensified.

Eight years after Chrissy was sold to Charlton for a £75,000 profit on the basis that his best days were probably behind him, the left-back was still playing Premiership football with Watford at the age of 37. The fact that he won the last of his five England caps in 2002 rather demonstrates that, on this occasion, the Bald Eagle's judgment was about as steady as Chrissy's right peg.

The irony is not lost on Chrissy. 'Yes, it came like a bolt out of the blue,' he tells me. 'We were settled in Derby and absolutely loved the East Midlands. I mean, little things like finally getting to know your way around the city were really important. Sometimes I look back and wish I'd stayed longer because we achieved so much, and hopefully I left my mark. Maybe it

Chrissy clears, watched by David Beckham, as the Rams take on Manchester United.

was meant to be. I don't look back with sadness because I went on to represent my country while with Charlton, but my fondness for Derby will always stay with me.'

He holds similar affection for Southend, the club he joined from Crystal Palace in 1990 and went on to play for more than 250 times over the next six years. 'I was captain at Roots Hall when Derby came in for me,' he recalls. 'There was always talk of me moving on, and at that time a transfer to Manchester City was close but didn't materialise. Just as well really, because they dropped through the divisions soon after. Then I spoke to Jim Smith about moving to Derby. It was a big decision but an easy one because Derby were top of the First Division at the time.

'But Southend were terrific for me. My first manager there was David Webb, who was a bit of a hero with the supporters, and he taught me my trade as a player. After a while you take it on yourself. You have to build a picture of yourself as someone who can become a top player and represent your country. Playing in Divisions Two and Three for Southend can make that dream seem a million miles away, but I am an example that it can be done.'

So what about the 'nice bloke' tag? Chrissy laughs. 'I would prefer to be regarded as a good player for whatever club I played for. I have tried to play in the shirt in the way the fans expected. You have to be honest with yourself as a player; the fans expect that. They want players to be passionate about their team. Wherever a team has achieved something – like we did at Derby and Southend – you have to remember it's not just the 11 that get you there. It's the players, plus the staff, plus the supporters. That's something I learned at Southend and carried on to every other club I've played for.'

I remind him that after a midweek defeat at Ipswich in the promotion-winning season of 1996, Derby's management and players steadfastly refused to take part in the customary post-match press conference...until a smiling Chrissy stepped forward as official club spokesman. 'The fact is it's a major part of a player's career to speak to journalists and supporters,' he says. 'More players should take it on, and media training for players is something I'm particularly keen on. After we lost at Ipswich I spoke because I understood that maybe Jim didn't want to say the wrong thing, but as a player I felt I could put my hand up and take responsibility.'

Those early months at Derby were tough. A replacement for Shane Nicholson, who wore the number-three shirt 23 times that season before joining West Bromwich Albion, initially on loan, in February 1996, Chrissy was thrown into a team riding high at Christmas, but suddenly stuttering in the new year despite the January signings of Chris and £1 million striker Ashley Ward. Part of the problem was that he was asked to learn a new role – that of wing-back – in Jim Smith's sweeper system. 'At that time Steve McClaren had introduced a sports psychologist at Derby called Bill Beswick. My problems in acclimatising at Derby makes it into a book Bill wrote. I had played left-back all my career, and I came into a role I was unfamiliar with and had no real time to settle into. It was especially tough because I was living in a hotel and trying to get to grips with the pressures of playing for a big city club.

'At Southend it was more laid back and you sort of felt you knew all the fans personally, but supporters' expectations at Derby hit me for six. What helped was us going up and then having a pre-season where I got to know the role. At the end of our last season at the Baseball Ground (the club's first in the Premiership) I was crowned Player of the Year, which was brilliant.'

That first Premiership season was a real humdinger during which the canny Smith brought in Croatian class in playmaker Aljosa Asanovic and defensive nous in the battle-hardened Paul McGrath to settle early-season nerves. There were home victories to savour over Sunderland, Leicester City,

Chrissy in action against Liverpool at Pride Park.

Chris Powell is Player of the Year ahead of the last-ever game at the Baseball Ground.

Middlesbrough, Coventry City, West Ham, Chelsea, Tottenham and Aston Villa, and of course that unbelievable 3–2 victory at Old Trafford when 1996–97 champions Manchester United were stunned by Paul Wanchope's debut wonder goal.

Chrissy received the Jack Stamps Trophy amid unparalleled razzamatazz ahead of the last-ever League game at the Baseball Ground on 11 May 1997. Arsenal were the visitors as a reduced-capacity crowd of 18,287 fans witnessed a 3–1 defeat at the famous old stadium. It marked a satisfactory season of consolidation back in the top flight, during which Chrissy played 39 times and, as an added bonus for Rams fans, Forest were relegated as the bottom club.

On to the new Pride Park Stadium, which remains one of Chrissy's favourite football venues. 'I remember Dean Sturridge teasing me that I was never going to score for Derby, but then I got that goal against Everton and wow! There really is no better feeling than scoring at Pride Park. I actually scored another in the Cup against Southampton – with the right foot too! You can't beat a full house at Pride Park. West Ham came close in my time there, but for pure passion Derby County supporters are the best.'

That first season at Pride Park turned out to be Powell's last as the Rams improved again, recording a ninth-place finish as manager Smith introduced Italian talent in the shape of the cultured Stefano Eranio and the instinctive Francesco Baiano. None of the left-backs in the following seasons, including immediate replacement Stefan Schnoor, ex-England international Tony Dorigo and Argentine Luciano Zavagno, achieved anywhere near the consistency of the departed Powell.

Pride Park cropped up again when England came calling as Chrissy picked up the third of his five caps as a second half substitute in the 4–0 thrashing of Mexico in May 2001. 'I was playing for Charlton and doing okay but had no inkling at all that I would be chosen for my country. Sven said he would look at every club and I must have been doing something right at the time. That's the pinnacle of any player's career, representing your country, and doing it at Pride Park made it extra special. It was truly incredible. I was getting the cheers because of the Derby fans and I remember thinking at the time, "You can't beat this!" That said, I wasn't just representing my country but all the teams I had played for, including Crystal Palace as a kid, Southend, Derby and Charlton.'

When I spoke to Chrissy he was chairman of the Professional Footballers' Association (PFA), still playing football and had never been happier. 'I enjoy being a role-model for the football community and meeting people,' he says. 'Whether it's trying to bring awareness of anti-racism or trying to improve facilities for supporters, I love it.'

Chris Powell? Yes, a nice man. A *very* nice man.

1997–98 **Francesco Baiano**

Francesco Baiano arrived in Derby just in time for the team photograph on the brand new Pride Park pitch ahead of the 1997–98 season, the Rams' second in the Premiership.

He missed meeting the queen, who had officially opened the new home of Derby County, and was introduced by manager Jim Smith to his squad. A grinning Lionel Pickering kept the Duke of Edinburgh occupied and also at the centre of it all was vice-chairman Peter Gadsby, the director in charge of the new stadium project who had first seen the potential of the former refuse site on Chaddesden Sidings.

The Queen was not the only famous name associated with the Rams that summer. Roberto Baggio, once the world's best player but now apparently in decline due to injuries, was linked with the Midlands club. In July another established Italian international, the stylish Stefano Eranio, arrived from Milan as a free agent after winning three Serie A titles and appearing in two European Cup Finals in his five seasons with one of the world's most celebrated clubs. Maybe the Baggio rumour was not so outlandish after all?

However, it was the lesser known Baiano, and not Baggio, who added still more continental flair to Smith's cosmopolitan squad as Derby set about improving on an encouraging first season in the top flight.

The variety of languages being spoken on the team coach was staggering and certainly bamboozled the Rams' Yorkshire-born manager, who always mispronounced his latest signing's surname as 'Baian-eeo'.

Francesco Baiano.

In goal was the Estonian Mart Poom (whose surname should have been pronounced 'Porm', though Poomy never minded), Danish defender Jacob Laursen, the Croats Igor Stimac and Aljosa Asanovic, Costa Ricans Paulo Wanchope and Maurico Solis, two Dutchmen in club captain Robbie van der Laan and Ron Willems and now the two Italians. Even English-born Darryl Powell and Deon Burton played their international football for Jamaica; indeed, later in his Rams career Burton became the club's most capped international, overtaking Peter Shilton's 34 England appearances while a Derby player. The Norwegian Lars Bohinen had also joined the ranks by the end of that 1997–98 campaign, and of course Rory Delap, despite his North

Baiano celebrates a goal against Aston Villa at Pride Park.

Baiano on the ball against Tottenham at Pride Park.

East accent, represented the Republic of Ireland (it was Rory, in all innocence, who asked me during the American tour of 1999 before we flew from Chicago to Denver where he could 'change his dollars into Colorado money…' He thought Colorado was a different country altogether!).

At this time interpreters seemed to be in as plentiful supply as coaches at Raynesway, and I always found it interesting how some foreign imports made a very determined effort to learn the language, while others were happy to get by.

By the time van der Laan arrived at Derby from Port Vale at the start of Smith's Derby adventure he already sounded more Potteries than Dutch, and his compatriot Willems also had a firm grasp of the English language.

The supremely confident Stimac had hardly a word of English when he arrived at the Baseball Ground in the autumn of 1995. An intelligent man, he threw himself whole-heartedly into learning the language but soon found that Raynesway English was not necessarily the Queen's English. Accompanying him on a community event soon after he signed from Hajduk Split for £1.57 million, I could only look on in horror as he patted a small child on the head before enquiring sweetly, 'How the f*** are you?' A swift de-briefing session was arranged.

The enormously talented Aljosa Asanovic, recommended to Derby by Stimac and snapped up in June 1996 before impressing for Croatia in the European Championships that same summer, was a canny chap. He steadfastly refused to speak any English, and with the now fluent Stimac at his side, there was little need.

The Guardian football writer Michael Walker was so determined to interview Asanovic towards the end of the midfielder's influential first season in the Premiership that he brought his own interpreter along after being told the player spoke not a word of English. Half an hour into a rather torturous interview Asanovic, growing bored, suddenly piped up: 'Listen, would it be easier if we did this in English?' My theory is that playing dumb meant he could answer Smith's tactical touchline rants with a shrug of the shoulders. 'Asa' always preferred to play his own game.

The German defender Stefan Schnoor was another confident individual who, after arriving from SV Hamburg in July 1998 insisted there was absolutely no need for an interpreter to attend his introductory press conference at Pride Park Stadium. 'Ladies and gentlemen,' Schnoor announced, smiling at the assembled media corps. 'First I would like to say I am very happy to be here at Derby County Football Club – and so is my husband...'

I do not ever remember Baiano giving English a try. The striker, only 5ft 7in tall, smiled a lot, but it was his compatriot, the charming Eranio, who took English lessons and became increasingly fluent. He was soon able to explain that Baiano's nickname 'Cicco' had been given to him because he was 'here, there and everywhere'. As for Baiano himself, he let his football do the talking.

New Derby County signing Francesco Baiano poses at Pride Park stadium.

Cicco, who played with sticking plasters covering the gypsy earrings he wore in each ear, had won two Italy caps in a career that had started at Napoli and included loan spells with Empoli, Parma, Avellino before moves to Foggia and Fiorentina, where he was part of the so-called 'Ba-Ba' strike duo with the more celebrated Gabriel Batistuta.

Not yet fit enough to feature in the inaugural game against Wimbledon, which famously was not completed when the new stadium's lights failed, or the two single-goal away defeats that followed at Blackburn Rovers and Tottenham, Baiano made his Pride Park bow at the end of August against newly promoted Barnsley. A twice-taken penalty meant Eranio became the first official goalscorer at the Rams' new home, although Ashley Ward, who had scored Derby's last League goal at the Baseball Ground, had initially claimed the distinction when he scored in the abandoned Wimbledon match.

Everton were swept aside next, and then Baiano opened his account in a defeat at Aston Villa on 20 September. For the next five games there was no stopping the Italian, who had an instinctive knack of finding the back of the net. Including the Villa game Cicco scored in six consecutive League games, equalling the club's record, a sequence that yielded three wins, two draws and goals galore. Cicco scored two in the 5–2 trouncing of Sheffield Wednesday (Derby's first win at Hillsborough since 1936) and was on the mark in a 4–0 home victory over Southampton and bagged two more in the defeat of Leicester City at Filbert Street. The little Italian was on the mark again, as was the leggy Wanchope, as the Rams earned a pulsating 2–2 draw against Manchester United – a game witnessed for the first time by a Pride

Baiano writhes in pain after an injury against Wimbledon.

Park crowd in excess of 30,000. Cicco's goal celebrations, posing cheekily by the corner flag as he waited for his teammates to join in, were becoming his signature, and he scored again in the next game, a 1–1 draw, as Wimbledon returned to Derby for the re-arranged fixture.

A 4–0 drubbing at Anfield in the next game was a reminder that, for all its style, Smith's Derby was not yet ready to break into the highest echelons of English football, though seven days later, on the first day of November, an ecstatic Pride Park crowd was treated to the 3–0 demolition of Arsenal, unbeaten at that stage and set to be champions that season with a one-point advantage over Manchester United. Although Baiano did not score against the Gunners, he buzzed around, elusive as ever, flicking balls past nonplussed defenders, prompting his fellow attackers Wanchope, who scored twice and Dean Sturridge, who bagged the other.

The artistry of Baiano in a fluid attacking three with the wiry Wanchope and the speedy Sturridge was a throw-back to the days of George, Lee and Hector, and an absolute pleasure to watch. Club captain Van der Laan told me: 'Cicco made so many things happen. He wasn't keen on learning English and we only got little sentences out of him, but we had good banter with him, and he was one of the reasons we were renowned as a team that could make anything happen on our day. That's what made that first season at Pride Park so exciting.'

Although Wanchope finished the campaign as top scorer with 17 goals in all competitions to Baiano's 13, the Derby crowd had been enchanted by the little Italian's wizardry, and it was he who received the Jack Stamps Trophy before kick-off at the last game of the season as the Rams finished the campaign with a flourish, beating Liverpool 1–0. Wanchope headed the only goal of the game from a Baiano corner.

In their second season in the Premiership Derby had improved by nine points and claimed ninth place. Sadly, the Derby crowd had seen the best of Francesco Baiano. Unlike the personable Eranio, Cicco never seemed to settle in the city and was a fitful performer as the Rams progressed again in 1998–99 with an eighth-place finish. He played fewer than half the League games, scoring four goals, two of which were penalties. After a dozen games of the millennium season he returned to Italy to play for Ternana then Pistoiese before his career dwindled out in Serie CI with Sangiovannese. He retired in 2006.

1998–99 **Jacob Laursen**

It was a joke in the media department at Derby County that if Jacob Laursen had not been a footballer he could have carved out a decent career as a professional hit-man. Jacob had that look about him – a steely glare, close cropped hair and a clipped way of talking which would have perfectly suited the phrase: 'Don't mess with me punk. You wouldn't like me when I'm angry, and I know where you live…'

Nonsense, of course, because Jacob was always an absolute gentleman in his dealings with the media and his teammates, though his ice-cool demeanour set him apart from the rest. Somehow, he seemed a lot older than everyone else in Jim Smith's Premier League squads for four years from the summer of 1996.

In a way, the defender from Denmark *was* a hit-man on the field of play, earning a reputation as one of the best man-markers in Europe. This attribute was just what Smith needed as his side took their first tentative steps in the Premiership. However, it was in the unlikely role of goalscorer (he scored only three times in 151 starts for the club) Jacob might be remembered best by many.

Manager Jim Smith again looked abroad after promotion to the Premiership in May 1996. Igor Stimac's Croatian international colleague Aljosa Asanovic arrived as the playmaker and Laursen, a Danish international, came in from Silkeborg. Both players were involved in the European Championship finals in England that summer, and in Laursen the Bald Eagle signed a defender who had won a League Championship medal in the Danish Superliga in 1993–94. He looked a snip at £500,000.

Jacob Laursen.

Laursen's debut for the Rams at the Baseball Ground on 17 August 1996 was eventful to say the least. It was assumed the Dane had been bought to play as a right wing-back – a position that had caused manager Smith much head-scratching in an otherwise highly successful 1995–96 season, but with Stimac not fit for the visit of Leeds United, Laursen played in central-defence alongside captain for the day Dean Yates, while a short-contract signing Paul Parker, formerly of Manchester United, started at right wing-back. The other debutants that day were Asanovic and

Jacob Laursen in the air as Derby County play Huddersfield Town.

Christian Dailly, also signed that summer from Dundee United.

After 18 minutes Laursen scored – but for Leeds. Lee Bowyer crossed from the left and the Dane, lunging to intercept, could only deflect the ball past Russell Hoult into his own net. When the visitors doubled their lead midway through the second half Laursen's debut was over as Smith sacrificed his new signing along with Darryl Powell and Marco Gabbiadini in a triple substitution that saw the introduction of Sean Flynn, Paul Simpson and Ron Willems. It did the trick: Derby scored two in a minute, the first a spectacular shot from Dean Sturridge and the second a rather fortuitous rebound off Simpson's shin as he chased down a clearance from Leeds goalkeeper Nigel Martyn. Although the visitors scored again, a second from Sturridge made the final score 3–3 and a capacity crowd of 18,000 had witnessed a breath-taking return to top-flight football.

A late Dailly goal at White Hart Lane four days later ensured Derby took an encouraging point from Tottenham, but a 2–0 defeat at Villa Park did little to inspire confidence for the first real stern test of life back at the top – the visit of Manchester United on 4 September. Once again a capacity crowd was at the all-seater Baseball Ground for this night match, but a stadium that had once squeezed in almost 42,000 was now painfully inadequate, and the new stadium slowly taking shape a mile away on Pride Park could not come quickly enough.

The emotions of the Derby fans that night were mixed: swinging from excitement to intense trepidation. United, who would walk the Premiership that season, had the imperious Eric Cantona to direct operations, the speed and trickery of Ryan Giggs and the impudence of the emerging David Beckham. They also had the world's best goalkeeper in Peter Schmeichel.

The previous weekend Schmeichel and Laursen had been on Denmark international duty together. Now they were on opposing sides, and after 24 minutes Jacob claimed first blood. Derby, playing towards the Normanton end, were awarded a free-kick when David May fouled Sturridge 35 yards from goal, just right of centre. It was a position that clearly appealed to the left-footed Asanovic, who in any case claimed the ball at all set-piece situations. But Laursen, after that disappointing own-goal debut, had a point to prove. He tells me: 'I stepped forward and for some reason fancied my chances. I told Asa (Asanovic) I was going to take it. He gave me the impression he hadn't understood me, but he eventually stepped aside.'

A Laursen glare is enough to make anyone back down, and the hit-man fired in a screamer of a free-kick that barely gave Schmeichel chance to move. As it rocketed into the back of the net the great Dane could only flap hopelessly around his left post.

Never one to let emotion get the better of him, Jacob did not over-do the celebration; but it was a satisfying moment. Thirteen minutes later he hit a poor pass to Darryl Powell that was intercepted by Giggs before Beckham demonstrated his shooting ability by beating Hoult comprehensively. It finished 1–1, but Derby fans went home that night knowing their team could survive in the Premiership. Smith's new signings were starting to impress and in Stimac, who had relished the battle with Cantona, Derby had a player capable of raising his game against the best in the land.

Laursen, meanwhile, was rarely as spectacular again in the black-and-white of Derby – he simply was not that sort of player. He got on with his job quietly and effectively. Indeed, his next headline-making contribution came at the end of January 1997 when he managed to injure himself in the warm-up ahead of an FA Cup fourth-round encounter at the Baseball Ground against Aston Villa. Paul Trollope was promoted from the bench, and Jacob's place at the back was taken by Dailly, who performed immaculately in the role of emergency defender, so much so it was a position he would go on to play for the rest of his top-level career at club level and with his country Scotland.

Laursen played 39 League and Cup game in his first season and chalked up 30 appearances as Derby improved again in 1997–98, chipping in with another rare goal in the early weeks of the season. Again it was a night match as the Rams travelled up the M1 to Sheffield Wednesday on 24 September. The home side twice took the lead before Derby, gaining confidence from the Italian influence of Stefano Eranio and Francesco Baiano, went on to win 5–2. Baiano scored twice, Paulo Wanchope and Deon

Jacob on the ball as Derby take on Bradford City in a pre-season friendly at Bradford.

Jacob is carried off injured by physios Gordon Guthrie and Peter Melville in a game against Aston Villa.

Swansea's Jonathan Coates chases Derby captain Laursen as Swansea take on the Rams in the FA Cup.

Burton had one apiece and Laursen drilled in a low shot to claim his second goal for the Rams. This was the time of champagne football, and three days later Smith's side scored four against Southampton at Pride Park.

It is a tribute to the reliability of Laursen – and the nous of the Derby crowd – that it was the Danish defender and not one of his more extravagantly gifted colleagues who was awarded the Jack Stamps Trophy in the Rams' most successful season in recent times. That season, 1998–99, Smith's side finished just short of the European qualifying places in eighth. The Derby manager was so confident in his rock in defence that he allowed Dailly to depart to Blackburn Rovers after just one League game of the campaign in a £5.35 million transfer that was the highest ever received by the Rams. The fee for a player who only found his true calling as a defender thanks to Laursen's injury 19 months before, might well have raised a half-smile on the craggy face of the Dane.

With the injury-prone Stimac now an increasingly peripheral figure, Laursen was vital at the back, starting 44 games in his Player of the Year season. The following season, 1999–2000, was his last as the cracks began to show in Smith's first full campaign without Steve McClaren at his side.

Domestic issues prompted Jacob's decision to move back to Denmark in the summer of 2000. He wanted to be closer to his children, and he went on to win another Superliga with FC Copenhagen in his first season, 2000–01. He returned fleetingly to England with Leicester City in 2002, just in time to see the Rams, for whom he had played such an important role in the best Premiership years, lose their fight for top-flight survival.

1999–2000 **Mart Poom**

Ask any member of Jim Smith's Premiership team their opinion of Mart Poom, and the question will be met with a wry smile and a shake of the head.

'Poomy was great,' the team's captain Robin van der Laan told me recently. 'We called him "The Machine". He was first on the training ground every morning and the last to leave. He would come in for lunch and almost be physically sick because he worked himself so hard. He was like the Terminator!'

Ask any of that same team why on earth Poomy allowed himself to disappear from view for three years as third-choice goalkeeper at Arsenal, and you are guaranteed another shake of the head and a shrug. Ask any Rams fan about Poomy's return to Pride Park with Sunderland in September 2003 and that last-minute headed goal and they will also shake their heads.

It was an unbelievable moment. The Estonian goalkeeper, Derby's Player of the Year in 1999–2000 and universally appreciated for his work ethic and enthusiasm, went up for a corner in an attempt to salvage a point and leapt higher than anyone to plant a perfect header past his opposite number Andy Oakes. Head down, seemingly embarrassed, Poomy sprinted back to his goal area, shrugging off the attempts of teammates who wanted to celebrate the miraculous goal. Poomy wanted none of it.

And still the Derby fans cheered 'Poooooom!' as the final whistle blew. Confusingly the chant always sounded like a collective boo, but Mart knew they were still on his side.

While manager at Portsmouth, Jim Smith had taken a look at this 6ft 4in super-athlete who could have had a professional career in basketball. Work permit problems meant there was to be no career for Poomy on the south coast, but in March 1997 Smith, in his first season in the Premiership with the Rams, paid the 'keeper's local club in Estonia, Flora Tallinn, £500,000 for his services.

Goalkeeper Mart Poom heading back to Derby after receiving his work permit. The Estonia star is pictured after arriving at East Midlands airport.

'My parents wanted me to play basketball because at the time it was the number-one sport in Estonia,' Mart tells me as he prepared for an international match in Slovenia (he has well over 100 caps for Estonia). 'Actually I think my mum was getting fed up with washing my dirty goalkeeper shirts! Anyway, I was too short for basketball, and I'm glad I chose football.'

Two days after signing from a club whose attendances barely touched 1,000, Poomy was blinking into the March sunshine at Old Trafford, surrounded by 55,000 fans. Opposite, in the Manchester United goal, was his all-time hero Peter Schmeichel.

At the time Derby were fighting for their lives in the top flight, and when Smith gave Poomy and another new signing, Costa Rican entertainer Paulo Wanchope, their debuts at the Theatre of Dreams, the best even the most loyal Rams fan hoped for was to avoid a humiliation. 'I was nervous before the game,' Mart recalls. 'I didn't know my teammates very well, hadn't worked much with the team and we desperately needed points. Then someone realised there was no goalkeeper's jersey for me! I'm told our kit man Gordon Gurthrie took one of Russell Hoult's shirts to the Old Trafford superstore and they somehow managed to black out his name and number and then print on my name and my squad number – 21. I still have that debut shirt – it's one of my treasures.'

While the Rams' only previous Premiership away win had been six months earlier at Blackburn, United, top of the table and European Cup semi-finalists, had lost only one League game at home in 28 months. Yet a Wanchope wonder goal sandwiched in between strikes from Ashley Ward and Dean Sturridge saw the Rams take all three points against Cantona and Co. 'A good debut always helps you to settle down, and that gives you confidence,' says Mart. 'I had supported Man United as a kid, and I still rate Schmeichel as the best-ever goalkeeper, so that debut was special.'

Almost as special, in fact, as Poomy's relationship with Rams fans. 'I was very happy and excited to

Poomy receives his Player of the Year award from Derby County legend Dave Mackay.

join Derby, and my best memories of my 10 years in England are there,' he says. 'They are loyal fans, but consistent too. In Sunderland, football is massive and passionate, but the supporters can turn against you very quickly when things don't go well. Derby's fans deserve another crack at the big time – it's a great club and I enjoyed playing at Pride Park. I was sad I was part of a team that was relegated, but I always follow Derby's progress.'

Poomy admits he is still as mad as a hatter on the training ground. Old habits die hard. 'I used to get stick at Arsenal because they had to give me the keys to the gym, but it's something I have always done,' he says. 'I don't see myself as naturally talented – all I have achieved has been through hard work.'

Now at Watford, Mart concedes he endured a frustrating time with Arsenal. 'The opportunity to join them came at a difficult time in my career,' he explains. 'I had established

Poomy in action against West Brom.

Back in the colours of Sunderland. Poomy pulverises Derby's Junior.

myself as number one at Sunderland but then injured my right knee and needed three operations. I missed almost 10 months, and when Arsenal showed an interest Sunderland still had doubts over my fitness, so I had to take the chance.

'Arsenal are a massive club, but I missed playing and had to accept I was number-three 'keeper behind Jens Lehmann and Manuel Almunia.' Not that Poomy had any complaints about the sheer quality of his teammates at Ashburton Grove. 'I worked day in day out with world-class players, and everything at Arsenal was focussed on quality,' he says. 'That keeps you sharp, but a big part of a goalkeeper's game is decision-making, and you can't practise that on the training ground.'

When Poomy finally decides to revert to being a normal human being and even adds a pound here and there to his wiry frame, this most personable of footballers is determined to give something back to football, and, more particularly, to his home town. 'I will definitely stay with football, probably coaching kids,' he says. 'I have taken badges already, and my other big project is to start a football school back home in Tallinn. I have identified a site for the centre and want to give something back to Estonian football. I have invested a lot of money, so hopefully it will be a success.'

No interview with Mart Poom is complete without a reference to that goal against the Rams. 'It was bizarre,' he says. 'I know goalkeepers go up for corners when their side is desperate, but I had never done it before. It happened in slow motion, and I don't think I have ever jumped as high – not even to catch a cross. Being back at Pride Park was a fantastic feeling, so much so that I didn't want to celebrate the goal. It was incredible to get a standing ovation from Derby's fans even after I'd done that to them. It shows the special relationship we had.'

2000–01 **Chris Riggott**

Chris Riggott is not the only kid who carried a milk crate into the Popside at the old Baseball Ground to get a better view of the action, dreaming that one day he would play for the Rams. But he is one of the very few who saw it through.

He has a vague memory of screaming Bobby Davison's name and, aged only five, watching Derby clinch promotion from the old Third Division with a home win over Rotherham United in May 1986.

Fourteen years later he was marking one of the world's great players, Gianfranco Zola, as he made his Derby County debut at Chelsea's Stamford Bridge; a dream come true. 'All I can remember is running around with a silly smile on my face thinking "How good is this?"' Chris tells me. 'Even though we were losing, it didn't matter because I was playing in a Derby County kit in front of the real Derby County fans behind the goal at Stamford Bridge…and I was just loving it.'

Chris and two other defenders, Ron Webster and Peter Daniel, are notable on the list of Jack Stamps Trophy winners for being born and bred in Derbyshire. And you would struggle to find a bigger Rams fan than Chris, who, despite playing his football at Middlesbrough, still retains two season tickets at Pride Park…just in case.

In his earliest days he sat in the top of the Baseball Ground's old Toyota Stand with his dad, uncle and three brothers. 'The first hero I can remember is Bobby Davison,' he says. 'The first team I really recall, though, is the one of Wright, Shilton and Saunders. I remember the cracking year we had in the old First Division when we finished fifth. That's when I can first remember loving it properly.

'I was in the kids' Key Club by then, which was in the Popside, though later it was moved behind the goal opposite the away end. I remember taking milk crates to stand on in the Popside – great memories! My three older brothers are all Derby fans too, and we all loved going to the matches with our dad.'

Rams defender Chris Riggott receives the Midlands Young Player of the Year award at the Raynesway training ground.

Like every other football-mad kid, Chris was originally a striker, but by the time he was attending St Benedict's School at Allestree he had dropped back to midfield. 'Benedict's was brilliant with all the sports facilities and the support the teachers gave me,' Chris says. 'The school played a big part in my development. I played for Derby Boys, but I didn't used to massively enjoy going to the Centre of

Excellence at Derby County because I used to find it quite serious and a bit pressurised. So at the age of about 14 I went back to playing at school, but after another year people were telling me I might have a chance of making it. I was playing centre-midfield at the time and Steve Round, who was Under-15s manager at Derby then, put me back to centre-half where he felt I stood the best chance of giving it a go. Thankfully and luckily I was offered an apprenticeship at Derby.

'There were other Benedict's lads in my year, and all were cracking players. Michael Lyons was regarded as one of the best players in the country in his age group at that time, but unfortunately for him it just did not work out. In football you need luck as well as ability, and you need people to like you at the right time. So far as I know, I'm the only one from my apprentice year currently playing League football.'

Eighteen months after signing as a professional for the Rams and two

Chris Riggott in action against Everton at Pride Park.

weeks short of his 20th birthday came the debut game at Stamford Bridge as a second-half substitute for another Derby lad, Steve Elliott. It was the last game of the 1999–2000 season, and it was just as well safety from relegation was assured, with Wimbledon, Sheffield Wednesday and Watford already doomed. 'We were 2–0 down when Jim Smith put me on,' Chris recalls. 'It was boiling hot and we ended up losing by four, but it could have been about 40! Zola was playing and I couldn't get anywhere near him.'

From 16th in 1999–2000, Smith's Derby slipped a place the following season, clinging onto their Premiership status. But a new star was born. Chris scored on his full debut in a League Cup second-round victory at West Bromwich Albion on 26 September 2000, and three days later he scored again in the League at Aston Villa. It did not take long for manager Smith to decide the local lad was a better bet in defence than two of his less successful imports, the Australian Con Blatsis and the £1.5 million Norwegian international Bjorn Otto Bragstad. Often playing in a back three partnering Horacio Carbonari and the dread-locked Taribo West, who made a 20-game flying visit to Derby from Milan that campaign, Chris went on to make a total of 34 appearances in 2000–01, scoring five goals, mostly from set-pieces. 'In the League I also scored at Tottenham and Chelsea, but at the same time we were conceding a lot of goals, so it was a bitter-sweet feeling,' he says.

Chris Riggott celebrates after scoring his first League goal for the Rams against Aston Villa.

The key game of the whole campaign was the trip to Old Trafford on 5 May. While Manchester United had already claimed the Premiership title with a huge margin over Arsenal and Liverpool, the Rams needed at least a point from the game to maintain a gap over the bottom three clubs Manchester City, Coventry City and Bradford City. Amazingly, United's celebrations were dampened as Malcolm Christie hit the only goal of the game, guaranteeing the relieved Rams a sixth successive season in the top flight. 'I still have a picture on my wall at home of me, Danny Higginbotham and Rory Delap taken after that game, clapping the Derby fans,' says Chris. 'That was a sweet feeling – in fact probably the sweetest in my time at Derby.'

As the Rams signed off with an inconsequential home draw against Ipswich Town on 19 May, Chris received the Jack Stamps Trophy. 'Being Player of the Year meant a lot to me, but it probably means even more now,' he says. 'That season was the breakthrough for me. My wife Emma was my girlfriend at the time, and she attended the awards night with me so all the photographs from that night are a special memory. I still have a replica of the trophy in my house at Harrogate. I have a place in Derby too because I go back all the time to see my friends and family, especially in the summer.'

While the next season saw the start of a new partnership in central-defence – Chris and big mate Danny Higginbotham each played 37 League games in 2001–02 – it was a season too far for Derby County, despite the much heralded arrival of former Italy striker Fabrizio Ravanelli. Jim Smith, refusing the offer to take on a general manager role, was replaced by his assistant Colin Todd in October 2001 and he in turn was given only three months in charge before the Derby County Board turned to a former captain, John Gregory. 'It just wasn't stable at all, not just with the change of managers, but with all the staff and coaches too. The fans don't really see that side of it, but there was a lot of disruption at the training ground. I really liked Jim and particularly liked Colin too, but he had a really tough job with no resources as the club tightened its belt. It was impossible really.'

As the Rams fleetingly fired on all cylinders after Gregory took over (they slipped away dramatically to record only one point from their last eight Premiership games), fellow strugglers Leicester City were swept aside at Pride Park on 23 February, Kinkladze, Strupar and Morris scoring in a 3–0 win. But Manchester United would once again be the headline game of the campaign. Sir Alex Ferguson's side arrived in Derby on 3 March, this time needing points in a title race that ultimately would be won by Arsene Wenger's Arsenal. Although Riggott and Higginbotham had terrific games against United's strike-force of Ruud van Nistelrooy and Ole Gunnar Solskjaer, it was Malcolm Christie who stole the headlines with two goals in a 2–2 draw – and he almost stole all three points. 'Manchester United at home was the stand-out game that season,' says Chris, 'and the fans still talk about the incident in stoppage time when Mally was adjudged to have kicked the ball out Fabien Barthez's hands. What I remember after that goal was disallowed is that United came down the other end, and I managed to block one which I like to think was going in. It was that sort of game – end to end.'

Derby County carried a huge wage bill into the lower League, and financial uncertainties off the pitch were matched by stuttering performances on it. 'I found it quite hard adapting to the First Division because it's a totally different style of football,' Chris admits. 'I was still playing at the back with Danny, but it was tough. When a team gets relegated everyone expects them to do well, but I can understand why it often doesn't work out that way.'

A Riggott goal in a 3–0 home win over Watford in December 2002 to add to his Derby County collection was the last highpoint. The following month he was told he was going to Middlesbrough. 'At the time I didn't have a choice in the matter. It was just a case of "you're going to talk to them". It was a massive wrench. Career-wise it was probably the best move, but I was sad to leave and I really didn't want to go. Just from a day-to-day life point of view I'd just bought a house and was living with Emma

Chris with the Player of the Year award.

Rams players Danny Higginbotham, Chris Riggott and Rory Delap acknowledge the travelling supporters after their 1–0 victory over Manchester United.

and we were happy in Derby. We were settling down, and then suddenly at the age of 22 I had to pick up everything and leave, but that's the way it goes with football. People reading this will probably say it's not too difficult with all the money that goes with it, but when it's your life it's a massive change.'

Whenever his Premiership commitments allow, Chris makes sure he is in the crowd at Pride Park. 'I watch every match I can and was there for the glory games when we were pushing for promotion last time,' he says, 'especially the Play-off Final, which was just a great day out. I went with all my friends from school and the family. I still have a couple of season tickets, which my family use most of the year.'

Towards the end of an injury-plagued 2007–08 season at Middlesbrough, Riggott went out on loan to help Stoke City towards an unexpected promotion to the top flight. 'The first thing I thought was "Great – I can live in Derby!".'

As we spoke, Chris was reporting back for pre-season training with Middlesbrough and admitted, with two years remaining on his contract, 2008–09 was an important season. 'I want to get off to a good start. I have learned now not to take anything for granted,' he said.

'My brothers tell me whenever I'm linked with a move back to Derby, which apparently happens quite a lot! To say I have fond memories of Derby would be a huge understatement because I love the place and I love the club. It would be nice to think I could play for Derby again one day.

'After playing in that first match against Chelsea I knew that no matter what else happened in my life I had achieved my dream of playing for my club. Anything after that was a bonus.'

2001–02 **Danny Higginbotham**

It speaks volumes for the decline that was setting in at Pride Park during the Rams' fifth season in the Premiership that Danny Higginbotham played his first game for Derby alongside fellow debutants Con Blatsis, Bjorn Otto Bragstad and Simo Valakari.

Of those four who turned out in a 2–2 home draw against Southampton in the first game of the 2000–01 season, only Danny can lay any claim to significant achievement in the black-and-white. He is also the first to admit a polite description of his first match for the Rams – indeed his entire first season – was that it was 'a learning experience'.

Danny went on to play just shy of 100 games for Derby County, but it all started with Branko Strupar and Deon Burton scoring the goals that saved the Rams' blushes after they went 2–0 down to the Saints on that 2000–01 opening day. Danny was, he admits, given a bit of a run-around by Kevin Davies while Hassan Kachloul scored twice for a Southampton side that included Matt Oakley, destined to lead Derby to Play-off glory at Wembley in 2007.

'It's true, I didn't make the greatest of starts,' Danny tells me. 'I was still playing left-back at that time, but as the season progressed things got better. I had to learn very quickly.'

He could be forgiven an unsteady start. While his move to Derby in the summer of 2000 represented a new challenge, it was also effectively the end of a boyhood dream. Manchester-born and a lifelong United fan, he had been an apprentice at Old Trafford and rubbed shoulders with Beckham, Giggs, Scholes and the Neville brothers. Wes

Danny Higginbotham applauds the fans after the final whistle during a Stoke City versus Derby County match.

Danny Higginbotham and Simo Valakari with manager Jim Smith after signing for the Rams.

Brown rose through the ranks at the same time, but Danny's first-team chances were restricted to just four games. 'My entire family are United supporters and my ambition was always to make it at Old Trafford, but the competition of course was intense. Sir Alex [Ferguson] was brilliant because he always made sure you did things properly. I was fortunate enough to learn the United way for a couple of years, and it was a great experience. Even with all those famous names, there were no big-time Charlies on the training pitches.

'It might sound like a big decision when Derby came in for me that summer, but Sir Alex rang me and made it pretty clear that it was best for my career to make the move. So I flew out to Spain to see Jim Smith and did the deal.'

The Manchester United boss and the Bald Eagle were big mates and Danny immediately enjoyed the atmosphere at Pride Park Stadium. 'Jim was always larger-than-life – a real character,' says Danny. 'You look at what he achieved at Derby and some of the players he attracted to the club over the years and he deserves a lot of credit.'

Announced as the left-back who would take over from the newly-departed Tony Dorigo, Danny found it difficult to settle in that role as the Rams endured a sluggish start to the 2000–01 campaign, taking 14 games to record a first win. 'I sort of stumbled across the centre-back role in training,' he recalls. 'Jim was playing three at the back and gave me the chance to slot in, and I really enjoyed it.'

The Rams manager was spoilt for choice as Horacio Carbonari, mid-season signing Taribo West and the eventual Player of the Year Chris Riggott competed with Danny for three positions at the heart of the defence. By the time Derby registered their first League victory of the season against Bradford City in November, Blatsis and Bragstad had disappeared without trace.

The highlight of Danny's first season was the return to Old Trafford for the penultimate game of the campaign. United were already champions and 67,500 packed into the Theatre of Dreams to anticipate the mauling of a side desperate for points to stay out of the bottom three. 'That was a special match,' says Danny. 'United had already thrashed us 3–0 at Pride Park, and no one expected us to get anything out of it. But Mally Christie scored a cracker that won the game for us. It was a fantastic result.'

So Derby survived at the expense of Bradford City, Coventry City and Manchester City and braced themselves for another battle in 2001–02. All seemed well as Fabrizio Ravanelli arrived to make a goalscoring debut in a home win over Blackburn on the opening day of the season. Too good to be true? You bet!

It turned out to be the last League win of Jim Smith's Derby career. He was relieved of his services in the October to be replaced by his assistant Colin Todd, who in turn was replaced by John Gregory in the new year. For the first time in their history Derby County had three managers in a single season and, for good measure, between them Smith, Todd and Gregory fielded a total of 34 players. The writing was on the wall. There was to be no survival act this time around as the Rams slipped out of the top flight.

A reassuringly constant feature in the centre of defence was Danny, who missed only one game all season and was the fans' choice as Player of the Year. That was at least some consolation, as was the

Danny Higginbotham during a Derby County versus Reading game.

Danny gets the better of Manchester United's Dwight Yorke.

scintillating 2–2 home draw against Manchester United in March 2002, when Christie claimed both goals and had a late 'winner' controversially disallowed when he nicked the ball from the hands of goalkeeper Fabien Barthez. 'Even after Jim Smith went, I still thought we had enough to get out of trouble,' says Danny, 'but it wasn't to be. John Gregory sat me down in the summer and talked through his plans and I made it absolutely clear that having been part of a relegation team I wanted to stick around and help us get back into the Premiership. That's how we left it.'

However, there was to be no instant return to the top flight. Danny signed off from another season of struggle with a penalty in the 1–0 home win against Brighton in the December and took a more straightforward route back into the Premiership by joining Southampton on loan, a deal that became permanent at the end of the 2002–03 season. 'Southampton were on a great run at that time, and when they came in for me Derby were happy to let me go, so I grabbed the opportunity,' says Danny.

Three years on the south coast were followed in August 2006 by a move to Stoke City. Made club captain in February 2007 after Michael Duberry's departure to Reading, Danny ironically had to watch Derby and Southampton battling it out in the semi-final of the Play-offs at the end of that season as the Potteries club were edged out of a top-six place.

Higginbotham, however, had not given up on top-flight football and a former United teammate, Roy Keane, gave him the chance to play on the big stage again with Sunderland, signing Danny from Stoke for £2.5 million just before the August transfer deadline in 2007.

2002–03 **Georgiou Kinkladze**

Never has a Derby County player received the Jack Stamps Trophy after featuring in as few games as Giorgi Kinkladze did in a season of struggle in 2002–03. The mercurial Georgian international started only 22 League games and was a substitute six times, scoring four goals, as chairman Lionel Pickering's ailing administration began to creak after relegation from the Premiership.

Carrying a huge wage burden into the First Division, not least that of fading Italian striker Fabrizio Ravanelli, the Rams' financial plight was such that Mart Poom was loaned to Sunderland in November 2002 and two of the club's brightest young talents, Chris Riggott and Malcolm Christie, disappeared to Middlesbrough early in the new year, apparently for a fraction of their market value.

Manager John Gregory, who had ambitiously placed Ravanelli on the transfer list in the summer before the season began (despite the striker having a year of his lucrative contract to run), was mysteriously suspended in March 2003 after the Rams had endured their fifth defeat in a row, a depressing run that had included a 3–0 reversal at Nottingham Forest's City Ground on 19 March. Allegations of serious misconduct against Gregory were never proved, and the subsequent board at Derby County paid compensation to the former player who lasted only 13 months in the hottest of hot seats.

Kinky in action against Preston on 8 March 2003.

There was a real fear that a squad assembled in a failed attempt to avert relegation from the Premiership might slip through the second tier as well. Something was not right, as the Rams started the season with a star-studded cast including Kinkladze, Ravanelli, former England internationals Warren Barton and Rob Lee and Scottish midfielder Craig Burley. Also still on the books when the season kicked off with an encouraging 3–0 home win over Reading were strikers Lee Morris and injury-plagued Branko Strupar, for whom Jim Smith had paid a combined fee of £5 million, and defender Horacio Carbonari.

Kinkladze, or 'Kinky' as he was known to the Derby fans, had to wait until the sixth

171

Georgiou Kinkladze.

League game of the season – a 2–0 home win over Stoke City on the last day of August – to get on from the bench as a substitute for Adam Murray. He had not figured at all in Gregory's plans up to that point but, coming on after an hour with the game scoreless, helped to transform Derby's performance as Christie helped himself to two late goals. Kinky was a substitute again 10 days later, coming on for Adam Bolder in a 3–1 win in the first round of the League Cup at Mansfield Town. The diminutive midfielder must have looked around the 5,788 crowd at Field Mill that night and wondered what his career had come to.

The darling of the Maine Road crowd during a dazzling spell at Manchester City from 1995 to 1998, Kinky had the world at his talented feet. Famed for his dribbling skills and outrageous goals, he was already a Georgian international when he joined City from his home-town club Dinamo Tbilisi. Despite winning the Manchester club's Player of the Year award in two consecutive seasons, individual brilliance did not translate to a rounded team performance, and City were relegated twice before Kinky joined Ajax in 1998. He hardly kicked a ball in Amsterdam and joined Jim Smith's Derby, initially on loan, in November 1999.

Smith had lost his innovative assistant Steve McClaren to Manchester United in February 1999, and after three solid seasons in the top flight Derby were starting to struggle, despite investing heavily in Seth Johnson, Burley and Strupar, each of whom cost £3 million, Lee Morris and an Argentine striker by the name of Esteban Fuertes, who allegedly had Italian ancestry and hence qualified for a EU passport. Fuertes made his last of eight League appearances for the Rams in the same month Kinkladze arrived. He was refused re-entry at Heathrow Airport after a club training break in Portugal on the discovery that his passport was forged.

I remember meeting Kinky for the first time at the old Raynesway training ground soon after his arrival. Everyone at the club had seen the promotional video touted by Kinky's agent that showed the talented midfielder in a blur of goalscoring action wearing the light blue of Manchester City. He was fast, slight, impossible to tackle and looked like an absolute world-beater.

The Giorgi Kinkladze I was introduced to, sitting quietly in a corner of the inadequate first-team dressing room at Raynesway, looked anything but a world-beater. Clearly overweight, and self-consciously so, he was also painfully shy and in a small voice explained for my benefit that he never did any TV interviews. He was scared of the camera, he said. Indeed, I do not recall Kinky doing any kind of media interview throughout his time with the Rams. It was nothing to do with him being 'big-time' in the modern parlance; Kinky simply found it impossible to talk to people he did not know.

There was much training ground work to be done before Kinky would be fit enough to find his feet at Derby, but manager Smith could not resist throwing him on for his debut as a substitute in a 2–1 defeat by Arsenal at Highbury on 28 November 1999. He replaced another newcomer, the Israeli midfielder Avi Nimni, and a couple of signature dribbles raised the spirits of the travelling Derby fans despite a third successive defeat in a tricky sequence of games against Liverpool, Manchester United and now Arsenal. There was no respite the following week as Leeds United visited Pride Park, sneaking a single-goal victory thanks to Harry Kewell's last-minute extravagant dive in the Derby penalty area. It spoiled Kinky's home debut and the Rams, in the bottom three, had lost in consecutive League games to the four teams that took the top four places in the Premiership that season, with Ferguson's United, now coached by McClaren, romping home with an 18-point advantage over Arsenal in second place.

For Derby, survival was the aim, and eventually finishing above Bradford City and the three relegated clubs, Wimbledon, Sheffield Wednesday and Watford, was good enough. Injury held back Kinky's impact, and Derby fans really only saw a fully fit Kinkladze for the first time in the February of the new millennium. His only goal of the campaign, the opener in a comprehensive 4–0 Pride Park hammering of Wimbledon, was worth waiting for. In the 65th minute, a pass from Rory Delap sent Stefano Eranio chasing down the right wing. His low cross was laid off by Christie for Kinky to swerve a delightful shot into the bottom corner of goalkeeper Neil Sullivan's net. Injured soon afterwards, the Georgian left the pitch to a standing ovation, but he had done enough to persuade the Rams to make his £3 million transfer from Ajax permanent that April.

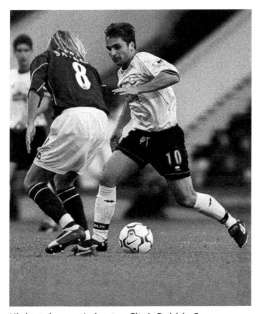

Kinky takes on Leicester City's Robbie Savage.

The issue that perplexed Jim Smith and subsequent managers at Pride Park – Colin Todd, John Gregory and George Burley – was how best to employ Kinkladze's undeniable, but unpredictable, talent. Over the next two campaigns, the second of which ended in relegation, Kinky was never a regular, scoring on only two occasions in a total of 26 League starts and being used an additional 22 times as a substitute. Smith, deciding Kinky was perhaps not the man to battle in the heart of the midfield where he could best influence the play, often used him wide on the right, a position that at least gave the left-sided magician the opportunity to jink inside.

Chris Riggott, who broke through into the first team during Kinkladze's Derby days, told me: 'He was probably the best player I ever played with, especially in training. His technique

Kinky rides a challenge against Newcastle United at Pride Park.

and ability were incredible. He was brilliant but sometimes blew hot and cold in matches.'

So, back to his Player of the Year campaign, and the statistics reveal it was definitely Kinky's most successful season. He scored four goals in 22 League starts, and three wins in April under new caretaker manager Burley (Kinky started in each of the victories) calmed relegation fears.

Paul Boertien, an honest pro who played more League games than any other Derby player in 2002–03 (twice as many as Kinkladze in fact), might have been in with a shout for the Jack Stamps Trophy in any other campaign, but the Rams supporters loved Kinky. Diffident as ever, he awkwardly received the award before an embarrassing 4–1 last game home defeat at the hands of Burley's former club Ipswich Town.

Confirmed as the full-time manager during that summer of 2003, Burley made it clear Kinkladze was surplus to requirements, and the little Georgian never played for the club again. He eventually joined Cypriot outfit Anorthosis Famagusta in 2004, winning the last of his 55 Georgia caps there before finishing his career at Russian club Rubin Kazan in 2006.

2003–04 **Youl Mawéné**

The big-money signings that characterised the Rams' frantic attempts to retain Premiership status as the new millennium dawned rather overshadowed a peripheral strategy by manager Jim Smith and chairman Lionel Pickering: to buy for the future.

So alongside the arrival of Craig Burley, Seth Johnson, Branko Strupar, Giorgi Kinkladze and Fabrizio Ravanelli were the lesser known Paul Boertien, Adam Bolder and Richard Jackson, all plucked from the lower Leagues. Another 'one for the future' was the French defender Youl Mawéné, just turned 21 when he was signed by Smith from Lens in August 2000. The £500,000 fee reflected the fact that Mawéné had featured in a successful side that reached the semi-finals of the UEFA Cup in 1999–2000.

The emergence of former apprentice Chris Riggott and the signing of Taribo West meant the millennium year was almost at an end before Derby fans caught their first sight of the central-defender, who made his debut in a 1–0 defeat at Southampton on 30 December.

Yet if Mawéné was one for the future, what a future it turned out to be, culminating in an acrimonious departure from Derby, under new ownership, as the 2003–04 Player of the Year.

Equally comfortable at right full-back, Mawéné made seven League appearances and two in the FA Cup in that first season and was growing in confidence as a regular choice in 2001–02 under both Smith and his replacement in the October, Colin Todd. His only goal in a Derby shirt came that November in a 1–0 home win over Southampton – and it was bizarre. The Saints' James Beattie sliced a clearance from a Craig Burley corner nearly 30ft into the air, and goalkeeper Paul Jones and his bemused defenders simply stood and watched, believing the ball was spiralling down behind the bar. Instead, it dropped on the line and spun back for Youl to make sure with the final touch. If that was a lucky break for the Frenchman, what followed was anything but as injury struck during the Christmas campaign.

Frenchman Youl Mawéné signing at Derby County's Pride Park Stadium.

Darryl Powell, Malcolm Christie, Youl Mawéné and Chris Riggott celebrate after Christie's goal against Bolton Wanderers.

The comeback he attempted at Charlton a month later was ill-advised. Playing under coach Billy McEwan, in temporary charge following Todd's dismissal, and with manager-in-waiting John Gregory watching from the stands, an injury sustained in the game meant that Youl would not be seen at all during Gregory's 13-month reign as he recuperated from serious knee surgery. Indeed, it was not until the first day of November 2003, fully 22 months after his previous Rams appearance, that Mawéné was picked by George Burley to deputise for Dave Walton, a giant of a centre-half signed by the Scot that summer from Crewe Alexander to shore up a leaky defence that had conceded 74 goals in the first season back in Division One. Walton managed only three starts in his Derby career, and it was a resurgent Mawéné whose classy defensive qualities helped stave off the very real threat of relegation as the Rams finished above only Gillingham and the bottom three clubs Walsall, Bradford City and Wimbledon.

Ten days before Mawéné's comeback game, Lionel Pickering, the club's owner for the previous 12 years, had been deposed. The self-made local newspaper tycoon who had thrown his own cash at his home club, initially to no avail under Arthur Cox but then to wonderful effect when the money was recycled by the wheeler-dealing Jim Smith, had sought to match the hungry ambition of Derby fans during the Premiership years. The thing about Lionel was that he was a *fan*, and if he sometimes listened to the wrong people it was only because he desperately wanted success for his club. He had reluctantly agreed to leave the Baseball Ground he loved – the place he had watched his all-time favourite player Peter Doherty in the post-war years – and, although his vice-chairman Peter Gadsby was the driving force behind the building of Pride Park, the new home of Derby County will always be associated with Lionel. Quite right too.

Carrying a huge wage burden into the First Division in the summer of 2002 and massively in debt to the banks, he was persuaded the way ahead was to ride out the financial problems and retain all the best players. In this way, he was assured, Derby would bounce straight back into the cash-rich Premiership. So players who might have attracted a decent fee before the transfer deadline closed that August – the likes of Mart Poom, Chris Riggott and Malcolm Christie – were retained, only to be picked off for peanuts by the time a poor new season was halfway through.

Quick-tempered and fiercely loyal towards Smith, Pickering had reacted publicly to criticism of the manager early in the club's fourth Premiership season. Some fans were disenchanted at only two wins in the first seven games of 1999–2000, phoning the Monday night *BBC Radio Derby* phone-in to say Smith was no longer the man to take the club forward. Pickering snapped back that those fans who called phone-ins and whose memories were short enough to forget just how much Smith had achieved at Derby should take themselves off down the A52 to support Forest.

Pickering had a point. Unfortunately for him, his timing was out. The next match was a 5–0 Pride Park thumping by Sunderland. The media, smelling blood, took the opportunity to spin the chairman's controversial quote into a call by Pickering for all Derby fans not happy with the club's progress to go off and support Forest, and from then until the day he died in 2006 he rarely spoke publicly, as some angry fans, proving that their memories were indeed short, demanded that now his own cash had been spent Pickering should make way for someone with real money.

On Monday 20 October 2003 Derby County was placed into Administrative Receivership for less

Youl Mawéné signing for Derby County with manager Jim Smith and club secretary Keith Pearson at Pride Park Stadium.

Youl Mawéné receives his Player of the Year award from George Burley.

Youl on the ball at Pride Park in a match against Wimbledon.

than half an hour and bought by a company calling itself Sharmine Limited. The new owners were John Sleightholme, Jeremy Keith and Steve Harding, and the following February Keith admitted the 'Three Amigos', as they became known, had paid only £3 for the club.

On the field of play, the loan signing of Leon Osman from Everton, criticised in many quarters at the time by those who felt a struggling Derby needed experience rather than potential, proved a masterstroke by Burley, while the much-travelled Paul Peschisolido was an instant hit, scoring the winner on his debut against Rotherham on 13 March and famously claiming two in a memorable match for Rams fans – the 4–2 Pride Park victory over Forest seven days later. One of his strikes that windy afternoon was credited to a plastic coffee cup that blew onto the pitch and bamboozled the Forest 'keeper into a mis-hit clearance straight to the feet of the Canadian striker!

Safety was not assured until Adam Bolder and Marco Reich scored the goals in a 2–0 home win against Millwall on 1 May, the day Mawéné was announced as Player of the Year. Although he had started 12 fewer games than both captain Ian Taylor and the latest successful product of the Rams youth system, Tom Huddlestone, Mawéné's poise under pressure had impressed the Derby County supporters.

The four-year contract he had signed in 2000 was now at an end, and the quietly spoken and always-courteous Mawéné suddenly found himself at the centre of a row over his future. The new board of directors had appointed as their director of football a former players' agent Murdo Mackay, who offered Mawéné a two-year contract extension and then withdrew it, apparently because the 24-year-old defender had not responded quickly enough. The Professional Footballers' Association was called in to arbitrate and ruled Mawéné had not been given enough time to respond.

Youl's frustrated agent said at the time: 'We recognise the club wanted to move things along as quickly as possible, but we weren't asking for the world, simply a chance to discuss one or two points.'

Mawéné promptly signed for Preston North End, where he was Player of the Year at Deepdale in his first season; it was an unfortunate way for his Rams career to end. Clearly some in the Derby crowd had been convinced that it was the Frenchman and not the Derby administration that had handled the matter badly, for he has sometimes been given a rough ride on his returns to Pride Park.

However, he is always magnanimous, a case in point being when Preston visited Pride Park during the Rams' disastrous 2007–08 season and recorded the Lancashire club's first FA Cup win over opposition from a higher division in 30 years. And how.

Mawéné plays against Derby as Preston win the semi-final Play-off match at Deepdale in May 2005. The Rams player is Marco Reich.

After the 4–1 humiliation of his former club, Youl, back to fitness after missing the entire 2006–07 campaign with another serious injury, said: 'People may expect me to see this as personal revenge, but that is not how I feel. Perhaps winning here means a little more to me because of what happened, but I still think Derby are a special club. I had my ups and downs in the four years I was here, but overall my image of Derby is good and I take no pleasure in their problems.'

2004–05 **Inigo Idiakez**

It is probably a little unfair to say that dead-ball king Inigo Idiakez made his single most significant contribution at Pride Park Stadium when he missed a penalty in the colours of Southampton. In driving rain, the Spanish midfielder who had scored some cracking goals in just over two seasons with Derby County, fired his spot-kick over Stephen Bywater's bar into the huddle of travelling Saints fans behind the south goal. Over two legs of the 2007 Play-off semi-finals the two sides had finished all square. The Rams scored every one of their spot-kicks in the penalty shoot-out that followed and Idiakez, the most proficient dead-ball specialist on the pitch, missed his.

The Derby players linking arms together on the halfway line immediately leapt into the air, manager Billy Davies was not far behind and the Derby fans went wild with relief and excitement. The Rams were on their way to Wembley glory.

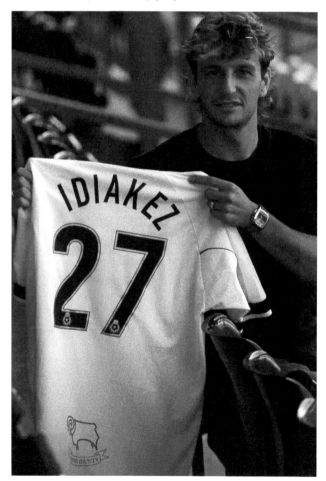

Inigo Idiakez signs for Derby.

Idiakez, meanwhile, was inconsolable, just as he had been at Pride Park exactly two years earlier when a scoreless draw against a Preston side managed by Davies had not been enough to prevent the Lancashire side, 2–0 winners in the first leg, progressing to the Play-off Final.

That night in May 2005 Idiakez had played through the pain barrier, as indeed had the Rams' other star of the season Grzegorz Rasiak. Both had missed the Deepdale leg with injuries, and neither was fit to play at Pride Park four days later, but manager George Burley, short of resources and star quality, played them anyway. It did not work out, and now both Idiakez and Rasiak, who scored a last-minute goal for the Saints in 'normal' time to take the 2007 semi-final tie into extra-time and penalties, were Southampton players and on the beaten side again.

Inigo Idiakez during a Derby County versus West Ham game.

After a season of incident both on and off the pitch during which ownership of the club had switched from Lionel Pickering to the 'Three Amigos' and George Burley had fielded 36 players in achieving 20th place in the First Division, the manager was determined to take a more conservative approach as he prepared for the 2004–05 season in the re-named 'Championship'. His squad would be smaller but would have more quality about it. His signings that summer certainly improved the quality: Tommy Smith arrived from Watford, Morten Bisgaard was a Danish international and Idiakez, signed from Spanish side Ravo Vallecano, was enthusiastically described by Burley in a media conference before he landed in Derby as 'a ball-winner who would add bite to Derby's midfield'.

Somebody had got his wires crossed, because the 30-year-old Idiakez was no tackler. His main talent was playing the ball to teammates and striking it with precision at goal. His record of 22 goals in 89 starts for the Rams tells its own story.

After odd-goal defeats in the opening two games of 2004–05 against Leeds United and Leicester City, Rams fans saw 'Ini' at his goalscoring best for the first time in a 3–2 Pride Park victory over Burley's former club Ipswich Town on 14 August.

The rangy Polish striker Rasiak arrived in late September to keep the other strikers in Burley's streamlined squad – Smith, Paul Peschisolido, Marcus Tudgay and the Brazilian Junior – on their toes. Although short of the class of runaway Championship winners Sunderland, Derby now had a team to be reckoned with and delighted a crowd of almost 31,000 at Pride Park on 11 December with a comprehensive 3–0 victory over bitter rivals Nottingham Forest. Rasiak scored two that day, both beauties, and Smith bagged the other. Forest, meanwhile, were heading down to the newly named League One – Division Three in old money.

A setback had come two weeks earlier at Deepdale when the Rams had gone down 3–0 to Billy Davies's well-organised Preston. Another came early in the February of 2005 when it was announced the club's rising star Tom Huddlestone, still a teenager, would join Tottenham Hotspur in the summer for a fee that could eventually be worth £2.5 million. The fact that the new owners of the club apparently needed to raise cash quickly prompted consternation among fans, not least the independent supporters' group Rams Trust, which presented a 110-page dossier to the media. By the end of the campaign the versatile Huddlestone, equally happy in central-defence or anywhere across the midfield, had played 47 times, more than any other player except Derby-born Lee Camp, who had claimed the goalkeeper's jersey as his own.

Going into the last scheduled game of the season at Pride Park on 8 May, both the Rams and their opponents Preston were guaranteed a place in the Play-offs but neither had a chance of automatic promotion. In short, there was nothing to play for and the likelihood was that the two Scottish managers, Burley and Davies, would lock horns again in the first leg of the semi-final seven days later. Before the game Idiakez received the Jack Stamps Trophy, and what should have been an energising 3–1 victory that day, thanks to goals from Idiakez, Smith and Peschisolido, backfired when the Spanish midfielder limped out of the game with a groin injury. Rasiak had

Idiakez during a match against Ipswich Town at the Portman Road Stadium in the Coca-Cola Championship. The final score was 3–2.

been injured in a defeat at Leicester 12 days earlier, and his season, which had yielded 17 goals from 37 appearances, was widely accepted to be over as he underwent a hernia operation.

Both the Pole and the Spaniard, who had contributed 11 goals that season, missed the Deepdale leg as Davies's committed Preston took a two-goal lead into the return fixture at Derby. The arrival of two exercise bikes in the Pride Park home dressing room on the afternoon of the second leg gave a clue that Burley was about to pull two rabbits out of his hat. Idiakez and Rasiak, both thought to be receiving treatment abroad, used the bikes to warm up their ravaged leg muscles ahead of kick-off, and their names were on the team sheet.

Their presence was not enough. Rasiak missed a late penalty and the Pride Park crowd were treated for the first time to the fist-clenched Billy Davies celebration that would become a regular feature at their stadium in little over a year.

The elegant Idiakez on the ball for the Rams at Pride Park Stadium.

Burley, meanwhile, had had enough. Always carefully unspectacular in his media comments, and in any case too much of a gentleman to go into detail, he resigned in June, describing his position as 'untenable'. Although director of football Murdo Mackay was also reported to have offered his resignation, he eventually stayed put, and the club's increasingly unpopular 'Three Amigos' appointed Bolton Wanderers' assistant boss Phil Brown as Burley's replacement.

Ini was top scorer with 11 goals from midfield in 2005–06 but lasted only until the last day of August in Billy Davies' first season in charge before being shipped out to Southampton for £275,000. The Spaniard was not the hard-working fulcrum the Scot wanted in his midfield, and the scene was set for an emotional shoot-out in May 2007 with Burley, now Southampton's manager, once again pistols-poised with Davies.

The Spaniard was a peripheral performer in a season of struggle for the Saints in 2007–08, during which they flirted with relegation and Burley left to manage Scotland. Idiakez was released by Southampton in the summer of 2008.

2005–06 **Tommy Smith**

It is a standing joke with Derby County supporters that the Player of the Year award is the kiss of death in terms of the recipient's Rams career. Cynics claim that once a player has his hands on the Jack Stamps Trophy, it is a near certainty he will be out of the door the following season.

Winger Leighton James, the ninth winner of the award in 1977, was the first to suffer this fate, shipped out to Queen's Park Rangers the following October by Tommy Docherty. Goalkeeper Roger Jones, winner in 1981, was on his way before the end of the following season. The great Archie Gemmill, belatedly Player of the Year in his second spell with the club, was released as he picked up the trophy in 1984, while prolific striker Dean Saunders took the award in 1991 and was promptly sold to Liverpool.

Defender Craig Short is another who received the Jack Stamps Trophy after his final game in a Rams shirt, and Danny Higginbotham was loaned out to Southampton as the reigning Derby Player of the

Tommy Smith during a game against Stoke City at the Britannia Stadium.

Year. Giorgi Kinkladze and Youl Mawéné, winners in 2003 and 2004, did not kick another ball for the Rams after winning the fans' vote. Steve Howard signed for Leicester City less than a year after experiencing Play-off glory at Wembley, and his predecessor as Player of the Year in 2006, Tommy Smith, headed back to his first club (Watford) on transfer deadline day in August of the same year.

Smith is a typical example of the way football has worked since the European Court of Justice's ruling in 1995 on the case of Jean-Marc Bosman, a footballer who, despite completing his contract with Belgian club side RFC Liege was refused permission to be transferred to French club Dunkerque without the payment of a transfer fee. The court ruled in Bosman's favour, declaring players should be free agents on completion of contracts, a decision that initially prompted consternation and panic in boardrooms up and down the land.

Tommy Smith, born in Hemel

Tommy Smith (right) during a Derby County versus Preston North End match.

Hemstead, was always destined to play for Watford where his father was on the academy staff. Spotted playing Sunday League football for Comets Sports club, Smith earned himself an academy place at Vicarage Road and broke into the first team in 1997, featuring in Watford's Play-off-winning side of 1998–99. During six seasons with the Hornets he scored 33 goals in 144 games, but after being dropped to the bench for the FA Cup semi-final against Southampton in 2003 Smith left the club as his contract ended, signing on a free transfer for Sunderland.

He signed only a one-year deal with the Black Cats, who were keen to retain his services after his lively contribution to a season that finished in Play-off qualification. But after 22 games Tommy was on his way again after being offered a three-year deal by Derby manager George Burley in July 2004.

Whether playing wide in attack or, occasionally, down the middle, the former England Under-21 international was always a first choice in both his full seasons with the Rams, scoring 11 times in 41 League starts in 2004–05. He was perhaps the only player in Burley's squad with the speed and determination to get behind his marker and was an instant hit with the fans, who admired his skill and work ethic.

I interviewed Tommy at his home in Findern during his second season when he explained how his father, himself a promising footballer in his youth, had been told by his own parents to give studies a greater priority than the sport he loved. Smith Snr, now a chartered surveyor, was determined his own sons (Tommy's brother Jack is also a professional, leaving Watford to join Swindon Town in 2005) would be given every chance to pursue their dreams. Tommy, though, is a bright lad who, had he not made it as a footballer, was keen to follow his father in the world of chartered surveying.

Smith's Player of the Year season was far from happy. First, manager Burley quit after the Play-off defeat to Preston, to be replaced by Phil Brown, in his first job as a manager. Polish goalscorer Grzegorz Rasiak, for whom Tommy had been supplier-in-chief during the previous campaign, departed for Tottenham on transfer deadline night.

All in all it was an alarming campaign during which Brown, who lasted only until January, and his replacement in a caretaker role, the academy manager Terry Westley, used a record 39 players. Inigo Idiakez was top scorer with 11 goals in a season in which the Rams were quick on the draw – 20 of their 46 Championship games ended all-square – while Smith chipped in with eight goals and played more League games than any other player, 43. He also scored from a penalty in an embarrassing FA Cup fourth-round defeat at lower-League Colchester United.

Smith, who normally kept his thoughts to himself, was angry enough after the last away game of the season had ended in a 2–0 defeat at Ipswich to have his say on the off-field financial turmoil, commenting: 'We haven't got too many excuses, but the lack of finances does have an impact. In terms

Tommy in action for the Rams against Norwich City.

of new faces, we've had to make do with loan players, who have not necessarily been exactly what we've been looking for in most cases.'

Before the last game of the campaign eight days later, when Sheffield Wednesday were the visitors to Pride Park, a local consortium of business people led by former vice-chairman Peter Gadsby had taken control of the club, and the future looked brighter.

Appearing on the pitch amid a fireworks display before kick-off, Gadsby, now chairman, and his fellow directors Mike Horton, Jill Marples, John Kirkland, Don Amott and Mel Morris, took their bow and Tommy received the Jack Stamps Trophy. A 2–0 defeat meant the Rams finished in 20th place in the Championship, and the task facing the new board, which had taken on a club with a reported £50 million debt, was enormous.

Smith, meanwhile, was on his way

Tommy recieves his Player of the Year award from former Rams star Stefano Eranio (right).

back to Watford by the end of August, as new manager Billy Davies, aware that the striker was entering the last year of his contract, accepted a bid of £500,000 from Adrian Boothroyd as the Hornets, promoted from the Championship in 2006 with Reading and Sheffield United, strengthened for the Premiership challenge. 'Tommy fits our culture – an attacking player who is athletic and quick and with a point to prove. He is a terrific signing for us,' said the Watford manager.

2006–07 **Steve Howard**

The thing about football fans is that we will sell our souls for success. The game we all love transforms sane individuals, completely professional in our everyday careers – be it surgeon or secretary, dentist or dustman, managing director or manicurist – into absolute monsters for 90 minutes every time our team plays. Football is an emotionally-charged pastime that turns today's heroes into tomorrow's villains.

When the final whistle sounded at Wembley Stadium on Bank Holiday Monday at the end of May 2007, victorious manager Billy Davies and his star striker Steve Howard were gods. The motivational Scot had done the impossible: transformed a pathetic relegation-threatened squad into a Premier League outfit in less than a year.

Howard, signed for £1 million at the start of the adventure, had proved the doubters wrong by bouncing back from a slow start to hit 19 goals for the rampant Rams. While he did not score in the Play-off Final, he played a part in Stephen Pearson's goal as favourites West Bromwich Albion were out-battled by a supremely focussed Davies team.

Only six months later both Howard and Davies were on their way out of the door at Derby County, and there were not many of us among the once-adoring fan-base begging them to stay. The hope of supporters everywhere is that the new man coming in – be it the manager, the centre-forward or the guy who prepares the players' pasta – will be better than the individual he is replacing and, using PR-speak,

New signing Steve Howard at Moor Farm Training Centre, pictured with Derby County manager Billy Davies.

'take the club forward'. This blind optimism is the reason why most of us go into games against even the most impossible opponents believing, hoping at least, that something miraculous might happen and our team might, just *might*, find a way of beating Manchester United at Old Trafford.

It also explains why even owners of pantomime-villain proportions such as Robert Maxwell in the 1980s and the so-called 'Three Amigos' in more recent times are always given a chance in the early days.

Managers and star strikers are, of course, well paid for what they do and have learned to ride with

Steve receives the Player of the Year award from manager Davies.

the fans' emotions, but I do wonder whether all of us were too eager to swallow the line that Howard, halfway through his second season at Pride Park, actually wanted to get out. 'When I came to Derby I was in the middle of my career, and I knew it was a big club and I wanted to sign, especially after talking to Billy,' Steve tells me. 'He was absolutely fantastic – the best manager I ever played for. His man-management skills were first class and professionally, on the pitch and off the pitch, he was the man.

'At first that season I think we all thought a mid-table finish would a decent achievement and scraping into the Play-offs would be a bonus. But as the season got going we started to eye automatic promotion, and I think it was just before Christmas when we really started to believe that we had a great chance.

'I didn't score in the opening few matches after joining Derby, but I didn't let it bother me and that was down to Billy really because he kept telling me he believed in me and told me to keep going and the goals would come. Those were the words of encouragement I needed, and I persevered, never let my head drop and started banging them in.'

His favourite strike of that first season was the late winner at Hillsborough on 23 September. 'The Sheffield Wednesday goal was probably the best I have ever scored,' says Steve. 'It came in added-time and was really important in terms of taking all three points, but of course I remember the Play-off goals too.

'We were underdogs against Southampton, who supposedly had better players, and it was the same story against West Brom in the Final, but we proved a team playing well together can beat a group of individuals.'

I ask Steve how he felt at St Mary's in the first leg of the Play-off semi-finals as he prepared to take a penalty that could give his side an all-important cushion going into the home leg three days later. The striker had already scored a well-judged header to equalise an early Southampton goal and now, just short of the hour mark, had Saints 'keeper Bartosz Bialkowski to beat from the spot. Even from the comfort of the press box at St Mary's I found it impossible to watch. 'It was funny, because I think I took four penalties in total that season, yet the most important, the one at Southampton that day, is the calmest I've ever been on a penalty,' Steve replies. 'My dad asked me after the game how I felt stepping up to take that one, and I told him I was surprisingly calm because I was so full of confidence and so focussed. Somehow I just knew it was going to go in. That's bizarre because if I'd really thought about it I would have realised just how much was at stake.'

Darren Moore's early goal at Pride Park seemed to settle the tie, but George Burley's side hit back with two goals before an own-goal put the Rams a goal to the good again on aggregate with time running out. Enter former Derby striker Grzegorz Rasiak as a Southampton substitute to silence the Derby crowd with a 90th-minute goal to take the match into extra-time. 'I was devastated when Rasiak scored for them right at the end of normal time,' says Steve, 'but I thought, "We've come all this way, and there's no way we're going to throw it away now". It turned our way on the penalty shoot-out, and when Idiakez missed his penalty I think all the players knew as a squad that we were going to go all the way. Again, I wasn't nervous taking the penalty in the shoot-out, and it was probably my best spot-kick of the season. I was well happy with that one, but even the young lads who took penalties that night did tremendously well.'

David Jones, Giles Barnes and Jay McEveley were also on target from the spot, and the new Wembley Stadium beckoned. 'Going into the Final so many people were telling me to take it in my stride and enjoy the occasion, but you are that nervous and so focussed before the game you really can't take anything in,' Steve tells me. 'But after the game, well that was different, and it's a memory that will stay in my heart for the rest of my life. It would have been nice to have scored at Wembley, especially as it would have been my 20th of the season, but I didn't care too much in the end to be honest because it was just a perfect day.'

On receiving the Jack Stamps Trophy, Steve adds: 'To get the Player of the Year award in that season, especially after not scoring in the first few games following a big move, is probably the best thing that has happened in my career. The fans are unbelievable.'

Much was made after that thrilling Play-off Final on 28 May 2007, about the lack of time it gave Derby to prepare for the enormous challenge of the Premier League, but at least Howard seemed to have acquired a new strike partner when Welsh international Robert Earnshaw arrived for a club record £3.5 million on June 29. On the big question surrounding Earnshaw's short stay before moving to Nottingham Forest – he started only seven League games throughout the entire season – Steve is as flummoxed as other commentators. 'I don't know if something was said, but as a group of players we were unaware of any problems and, like the supporters, we assumed Earnie would feature a lot more than he did,' he says. 'It's just a shame things turned out the way they did after such a magnificent promotion.

'Going into the Premier League season I definitely thought we were going to compete, and if things had stayed the same I honestly think that would have happened. Obviously a few things were said that we as players don't get to know about, and the board decided to get a new manager in and that didn't work. All I can say is I honestly believe if we had stayed as the same unit we would have got more points than Derby ultimately achieved.'

When Davies's side finally managed a win at home against Newcastle United on 18 September thanks to a superb debut strike from Kenny Miller, signed from Celtic, even the most pessimistic Rams fan would have hoped for at least a couple more three-pointers before the end of the campaign. But that was it.

Even when his mentor Davies departed, literally talking himself out of a job after his side were beaten 2–0 by Chelsea at Pride Park on 26 November, Steve believed there was still a future for him at Derby. 'Without a shadow of a doubt,' says the big-hearted Geordie. 'Don't get me wrong. Derby is my team now. It's in my heart and always will be. Billy Davies and Paul Jewell are like chalk and cheese, and when the new manager came in I think it's fair to say some players didn't respond in the way they should have responded.'

Davies's exit was slightly bizarre. Chelsea was the 10th defeat in 14 Premier League matches and the Rams were rock bottom having conceded 33 goals and scored just five. While Chelsea boss Avram Grant grumbled to media about the sending off of Michael Essien, Davies chose the post-match press conference to announce to incredulous journalists he had not had any conversation with chairman Adam Pearson in weeks. Undoubtedly pumped up by a more spirited display after the most recent home maulings his side had received at the hands of West Ham and Everton, Davies seemed intent on provoking Pearson. He was gone by the Monday.

In his first match in charge, new manager Jewell was denied a hard-fought draw as Sunderland scored late-on to take all three points at the Stadium of Light, and the challenge became even tougher seven days later as he took his side to Manchester United. 'No

Steve Howard goes up for the ball which is punched away by Birmingham city goalkeeper Maik Taylor during a Derby County versus Birmingham City match at Pride Park Stadium.

matter what happened in that season, no one can take the goal at Old Trafford away from me,' says Steve. 'I've a mate, Lee Howey, who used to play for Sunderland, who played in the Premiership for years and years and never scored. It's one of his biggest regrets, and I wanted to get that out of my system. I was determined I would score a goal in the Premier League, and to do it at Manchester United was just unbelievable.'

Just as unbelievable was the statistic that went with the goal: it was Derby's first in 777 minutes. On as a substitute, Steve slid in on a rain-soaked Old Trafford pitch to connect with Tyrone Mears's cross in the 76th minute. Already three down, the Rams, cheered on by away supporters who never stopped all afternoon, went on to lose 4–1 to the eventual champions.

A substitute again in a single-goal home defeat against Middlesbrough the following week, Howard realised another ambition when he made the starting line up at St James' Park the day before Christmas. A lifelong Newcastle fan and one-time season ticket holder, Steve could not find the back of the net, but goals from Giles Barnes and Miller secured a 2–2 draw and four points out of a possible six against the Magpies.

Howard's Derby career ended on 30 December 2007 when, non-typically for the ice-cool penalty taker, he missed a spot-kick that could have given the Rams a 2–0 lead over Blackburn Rovers at Pride Park. Brad Friedel saved his effort and Rovers went on to win the game 2–1. 'I got a phone call on the way back from the Blackburn game to tell me I was being sold to Leicester. I was absolutely devastated. I said I didn't want to go but was told the club had already accepted the bid, which told its own story – Derby County didn't want me. I arrived back at home and sat down with my wife, and we talked it through. The conclusion was that when you are not wanted you have no choice but to leave.'

2007–08 **The Fans**

It was not the way it was supposed to happen, but when the players failed to deliver during a Premier League comeback season that yielded only one victory, the fans decided to make their own entertainment. They continued to fill Pride Park Stadium and charmed the grounds they visited with their dedication to a hopeless cause and, perhaps most of all, their ability to laugh at themselves and their team. Even hardened national newspaper hacks warmed to Derby's never-say-die supporters, many claiming they were the best in the land.

The gallows humour started as early as the first match of September when Billy Davies's side were hit for six at Liverpool. Normally in such situations an ecstatic home support will start a cry of 'We want seven'. Instead the Anfield crowd could not help but applaud the visiting fans for their chant of 'We want one!' Later the same month as Arsenal took a 5–0 lead at the Emirates, the travelling Rams supporters struck up with an amusingly optimistic 'We're gonna win 6–5!'

At Old Trafford in December the Derby fans made more noise than the home supporters throughout, singing in the torrential rain, and when Steve Howard's unexpected goal pulled the score back to 3–1, they taunted the United faithful with an ironic 'You're not singing any more!'

By the new year the fans were no longer hoping for a miracle – the writing had been on the wall for a long time and it read 'relegation' – but they did expect and deserve wholehearted effort from the players they encouraged week in week out.

Too often the fans were sold short, and the Mexican Wave that sometimes swept around Pride Park as a disastrous season drew to a close, while humorous on the surface, sent out a clear message to the management of the club: Rams supporters were having more fun with a carnival gesture than watching the so-called entertainment being served up on the pitch.

Adam Pearson, having become the largest single shareholder the previous autumn when he bought out chairman Peter Gadsby, negotiated the takeover of the club in January 2008 by an American consortium managed by the Detroit-based General Sports & Entertainment. Pearson stayed on as chairman of football to construct with manager Paul Jewell a new-look squad in the summer of 2008 as Derby County prepared for life in the Championship. Loyalty should not be taken for granted, but Rams fans will have gone into another new campaign expecting their club to bounce back after a relegation season in which they were the only stars.

One of my last duties as a member of the Derby County staff came ahead of the final match of the 2007–08 season – a 4–0 home defeat to Reading, who also went down – when I managed to grab Roy McFarland for an interview before he made the Player of the Year presentation. Since receiving the new award in 1969 as Brian Clough plotted his assault on the best League in the world, McFarland had witnessed at close quarters the ups and downs of Derby County as one of 15 managers who succeeded the great man.

'You know it's hard to believe Jim, but it's 39 years since I was presented with that award,' he told me. 'I know the pain the fans have felt this past season, but the fact that they continue to fill this stadium tells its own story.'

And with that Roy Mac grabbed the Jack Stamps Trophy from the presentation table and walked out to the centre-circle to thunderous applause as the PA system burst into life: 'We are pleased to announce that the Player of the Year is. . .'

ND - #0301 - 270225 - C0 - 234/156/12 - PB - 9781780913827 - Gloss Lamination